For Beginners

By Electra Valencia

Follow @ HTTP://VALENCIACHARMS.COM/

Introduction

Spellbound you stare into the flame. Will my wish come true? You gasp as the flame flickers, is someone working against me, or is it just a draft through the room? You swallow hard as the flame sputters and crackles, what does it mean?

Everything in the universe is connected, as everything is energy. Learn how to tap into the hidden energies and change your destiny.

Candles are recorded to have been used from around circa 1200, for both good and evil. An Egyptian treasury official is rumored to have used a wax figure candle against Ramses III. Today, candles are an intricate part of many spells, from high magic with its extensive props and rituals, to Voodoo and Hoodoo with just the basic albeit sometimes shocking ingredients.

This book is for new or inexperienced practitioners interested in learning more about candle magic, and covers from selecting the right candle/s for your spell, the best time for your spell, adding oils and herbs, to interpreting candle flames. The basics of how candles work is covered, as well as incorporating tarot cards, runes, sigils and power symbols into your spells. Lastly, a number of spells that are easy to do but effective is included to get you started right away.

"All the darkness in the world cannot extinguish the light of a single candle."
- St. Francis of Assisi

Discover candle magic and make your wishes come true.

Table of Contents

Disclaimer and Legal Notice

This book is strictly for educational and entertainment purposes. Magic requires dedication, belief, and practice. No guarantee is given that your life will improve in any way using the information, techniques, and ideas given throughout this book. Results are dependent on the dedication and belief of the practitioner, thus will vary from person to person. Furthermore, the reader takes full responsibility and karma for using any of the information in this book. Magic is a tool to be used responsibly to assist you in your life.

Lastly, as magic is largely a belief system, the information contained throughout this book is subject to the interpretation about magic of the author, and may or may not be entirely accurate.

See **http://valenciacharms.com/books-by-valencia**

For formulas for famous blends such as van van oil, war water, goofer dust, florida water, court case oil, black arts oil, crown of success oil, and more, get my book ***Magical Blends***.

To discover what numerology is and how it works, as well as discovering more about yourself, others, and the world. See my book ***Numerology***.

Chapter 1: What Is Magic?

Magic is affecting the state of mind of yourself and others with willpower, thereby causing a change in the physical environment.

Candle magic is one of the oldest, easiest, and most widely practiced forms of magic, and is available to all to do. Candle magic is commonly considered to be either sympathetic magic (what you do to the candle happens in life) or petition magic (asking a deity to do something for you). In its most basic form, you require only one candle with no fancy rituals. In fact, one of the easiest and most versatile candle spells is to write your desire on a piece of paper. Read your wish out aloud three times, fold the paper up twice, and then place it under a tea light candle. Light the candle while thinking about your wish. When the candle has burned out, dispose of the paper or burn it for added power.

Many people do candle magic without even knowing it. Ever made a wish on your birthday and blew out a candle? That is candle magic where you either imagined what you wanted or asked a deity (normally your GOD), to grant you your wish.

So How Does Candle Magic Work Then?

A candle is a way to send energy and messages into the universe. You program the candle with your intention (either what you want or a petition to a deity), then charge the candle with power. When you burn the candle, the power you added to it, with the power of the candle and any herbs or oils you use, are released into the universe. That energy is used to change the universe so that your reality changes to your desires. The bigger the candle is, the more energy it has, and the stronger the spell potentially may be, as well as the longer your intention or petition is send into the universe.

Although there are hundreds of thousands of candle spells in the world, from all kinds of beliefs, they essentially fall into one of two groups.

Your Magic

In the first group, you send the energy to accomplish the spell. The efforts you put into the spell mainly determine if the spell is successful. You may add herbs, oils, and incense to add to your energy. But the success of the spell mainly rests on you. Here, focus, belief, intent, and imagination are key. You may ask a deity or god to help. However. Since you are doing the spell and sending your energy, the spell may succeed even if the deity chooses not to help you, if your energy is strong enough.

Pros:

Over time, you get stronger and your spells have a higher success rate. You do not need to ask a deity or god for help where you then owe them a favor or need to make an offering. You may become so efficient with your thoughts and energy that you no longer need candles to do spells. This will make you flexible in spell casting and save you a lot of money.

Cons:

It takes a lot of focus and a clear mind, as well as a lot of willpower to do a spell on your own. If you face someone who opposes you that uses powerful deities, you may lose badly. It may take years of dedication and practice to reach a level where you have a high success rate with spells. Doing powerful spells or several spells in a short time can drain your energy, leaving you weak or possibly causing you to fall ill.

A Petition Spell

With a petition spell, you are not doing any part of the spell yourself. The candle spell you do is asking a favor of a particular deity, ancestor, god, or even the universe, to go and do the task you ask of them. You may do it nicely by giving an offering and petitioning to their goodwill, or you may invoke an entity and force it to do your bidding. With this spell, it does not matter how much magical power you have. What matters is if your petition is accepted or your control over the entity worked, and if the entity has the power and the will to do what you asked for.

Pros:
You need no magical power to get powerful results. Spells to invoke powerful entities to do your bidding had been passed down through centuries and are easily available. Doing a powerful spell does not drain you. This type of spell casting is a favorite amongst professional practitioners who may do several spells in a day.

Cons:
If asking a deity for a favor, you usually owe something to them, even if only an offering. There is no guarantee that the deity will accept your offer or even that they will perform the asked tasks correctly. They may put their own twist to it, especially if your wording is not clear. Your deity may try to do the task, but your opposition may be using a stronger deity than yours, forcing you to abandon your request, or petition a yet stronger deity that may demand higher sacrifices for its services. If invoking a spirit, the controlling and commanding spell may fail, possibly causing the spirit to turn on you. An opposition may take control over the spirit you tasked, and turn it on to you.

Interestingly. The majority of people, especially those that say they know nothing about magic nor practice it, practice this kind of spell. Going to church and asking GOD to help you get the new job is a petition for a favor. So is wishing on a shooting star. Invoking spirits (especially if you allow them to possess your body) is the most dangerous spells there are. Depending upon the spirit that you invoke, they are also potentially the most powerful.

Chapter 2: Why Practice Candle Magic?

Do you really need a candle to practice magic? No. Magic is essentially all about intention and willpower that are directed or focused on a goal through imagination. Candles, herbs, oils, rituals, chanting and all that, are there to help you with your goal. Almost like training wheels on a bicycle. In honesty, the oldest of magic uses nothing but thought, and although almost forgotten by many today, is still some of the strongest magic around.

However. To make something happen by thought alone takes a lot of willpower, concentration, and belief in yourself. This is one reason why many practitioners turn to some form of ritual magic as they believe in doing spells that others have 'proved' to work. This may be okay for a start. However. You can forget that you actually need nothing but thought, and focus. You can end up with the belief that if a spell was not done exactly to the minute on the correct day with the moon in the correct state, and with the correct candles, herbs and oils, the spell will not work.

Candle magic offers an easy start on your path to practicing magic by thought alone, as the candles aid in focusing your energy and intent as well as creating a reference for you to visualize what you want. Candles are easier to use and cheaper than learning some exotic spells and words while dressed in an expensive outfit in a special room used only for magic. However. Even if you like high magic with its rituals and props. Candle magic offers an alternative for the times you do not want to, or have the time for a long and fancy spell.

Another benefit of candle magic is that you can get ready-made spell kits with all the items needed, often with charged candles. Charged candles are candles that are already dressed and charged for a specific intent (say protection or prosperity) by another practitioner. These are the easiest spells to do, as all you need to do is light the candles. However. You can add your energy to the charged candle to make the spell stronger. Candles can tell you the progress and expected results of your wish while the spell is in progress.

How Long Does a Spell Take To Work?

There is no exact answer to this. However. You should see some results in two to four weeks for normal spells like prosperity or health spells. Business success and love spells may begin to work immediately, but normally take a few hours to days depending on the spell. Remember. As much energy and focus as you put into your spell is as much energy as you will get out. Your energy affects the success of your spell. If you are tired or emotional, rather rest first, and then do the spell when you are in a better state.

Merging Energy

If you do spells that you found online, from books, or another spell caster, your energy merges with the energy of the spellcaster from whom you got the spell from. If your energy is not compatible with that of the other spellcaster, or the other spellcaster would never agree to you using the spell for the purpose you are using it for, the spell will normally fail or have weak results.

However. If your energy merges well, the spell will become far more powerful and success is far more likely.

If a spell does not feel right to you or fails, use it as a basis. Then change the spell and create your own that feels right to you.

Chapter 3: History of Candles

Candles have fascinated people and lit their path in the darkest of nights for over 5000 years. Yet; their origin is as secret and mysterious as candle flames are captivating.

Although ancient Egyptians used fibrous reeds, called rushes, and dipped them in animal fat to create torches (called rushlights) around 3000 B.C, the first use of a wick is often credited to the ancient Romans. They took rolled papyrus and used it as a wick, greatly improving the burning of the candle. The Papyrus was repeatedly dipped in melted tallow (animal fat) or beeswax to create a candle with the desired thickness.

Evidence has been found by historians that early Chinese used rice paper as a wick, and rolled it in insect fat and seed oil. The candle was often encased in paper tubes. Evidence has also been found of the Chinese using beeswax for candles as far back as the Tang Dynasty (618-907 A.D.) Early Japanese used oil from tree nuts as wax while Indians used the oil from the fruit of the cinnamon tree.

The Jewish Festival of Lights (Hanukkah) dates back to 165 B.C. and centers on candles. Candles fascinated even Constantine. In the 4th century, he ordered the use of candles during the Easter service.

Due to the price of beeswax, tallow (animal fat) and fat from plants were the widest used wax up until the Middle Ages when beeswax became more affordable and popular.

Candles became so popular during the 13th century, that candle makers (chandlers) took their trade to the road. People used to save leftover animal fat for the chandlers. They would come by the house and make candles for the household from the saved animal fat, in the people's houses.

In the late 18th century, candles became far more popular and easy to obtain. With the growth of the whaling industry, sperm whale oil was available in abundance (spermaceti). Spermaceti wax was obtained from the oily liquid within the head of a sperm whale.

A whaler had to climb into the head of a dead whale through an opening made in the head, and scoop out the oil with a bucket. The oil was often used in lanterns, as it burned far clearer than other animal fats while being cheaper than beeswax. Spermaceti allowed candles to be affordable to common households and became the first standard candle to be manufactured. Spermaceti wax is harder than tallow and allowed candles to be transported easier as it did not deform and melt as easily as tallow candles.

In the 1820s, French chemist Michel Eugene Chevreul discovered a way to extract stearic acid from animal fatty acids. Adding this to candle wax created a harder, more durable wax, called stearin wax.

Up until 1834, candles were made by hand, often by repeated dipping of the wick in melted wax. Joseph Morgan developed a machine that could mass-produce molded candles and eject the candles automatically. This resulted in candles being mass-produced, increasing availability while reducing cost.

Introduced in the early 1850s, paraffin wax is created by separating the waxy substance from petroleum and refining it. Paraffin wax is cheaper than any other wax available, as well as burns cleaner and more consistently than tallow wax. However. On its own, paraffin wax is too soft to be used in commercial candles and requires the addition of stearic acid. The cheap and easily obtainable paraffin candle caused a boom in the candle industry and dominated household lighting until 1879 when the light bulb was introduced.

Today, candles are more used for decoration, romantic settings, churches, and magic, than for lighting. With the development of modern machines and technology, candles are available in multiple colors and shapes, as well as the ability to add scent to them. Most of these are paraffin candles. However. With an estimated rise of at least 1% in demand for candles per year, and an estimated drop of 1.5% of raw materials for paraffin wax, synthetic and plant waxes are increasingly being mixed into candle making. A big drive is to replace paraffin wax with palm oil-based wax, which is a renewable source of raw materials.

Chapter 4: Candle Materials

In essence, a candle consists of a fuel and a wick to burn it. However. What kind of wick and what kind of fuel to use depend a lot on your needs. For the candle flame to burn correctly, the size and type of the wick need to match the type of wax and the size of the candle. Following is a basic explanation of candlewicks and waxes, to help you choose your candles.

Wicks

The wick controls how strong a candle burns, how fast the wax is consumed, as well as if the candle burns all the way down. There are several wicks on the market, with each one intended for a different use and or wax.

Wicks used today are commonly made of tightly woven or braided threads of cotton or other fabric material. The wick is soaked in a substance that inhibits smoking as well as making the wick fire retardant (mordanted). Adding fire retardant to the wick is essential as the wick would burn itself out before the wax of the candle could travel up the wick, and be used as fuel. The salts in the mordanting mix also cause the wick to lean out of the flame and curl back on itself. This allows the wick to be self-trimming, as well as burn up without leaving ash.

Before wicks are used for candle making, they are typically primed by dipping the wick into melted wax. This allows the wax to flow into the air spaces between the threads of the wick, and normally takes about five minutes. Priming gives the wick fuel to start with when lit. Once the candle is burning, wax flows up the wick, and priming has no effect on the burning of the candle, just the initial start. A wick that was not properly primed may struggle or fail to start a candle.

Some wicks, especially those in tea light candles, are tabbed before use. A metal wick sustainer tab is crimped onto the bottom end of the wick, to keep the wick upright when the candle burns.

Tabs may extend a length up the wick (typically from 3 to 10mm), to stop the candle from burning all the way to the bottom. This is often used in glass-encased candles to ensure that the flame does not burn down to the glass, and possibly cracking it.

Some candles, normally container and votive candles, come with metal-core wicks. Normally either a zinc or tin wire is used. It is twisted around or pushed through the wick to keep it upright when the surrounding wax liquefies when the candle is used. Note that lead wicks are officially banned in the United States since 2003, but may be available in other counties. The use of lead-core wicks are normally in cheap candles, do check when buying.

The size of the wick depends on the size of the candle. Too small a wick can cause the candle to barely burn or die. Too large a wick can cause an abundance of smoke and a large flame. The candle can also burn too fast, and mushrooming or knotting of the wick may occur (carbon buildup on the wick). Long or crooked wicks can cause the candle to burn uneven, smoke, cause drippings (wax melting away), or flaring of the flame (jumping up and down).

Although there are literally hundreds of types of wicks on the market, most of the wicks on the market fall into the following types.

Flat ***Wicks***

Flat wicks are normally made from three bundles of fibers that are flat-plaited or knitted together. This wick is the most commonly used today and burns very consistently, as well as curls into the flame to be self-trimming.

Square Wicks

Square wicks are braided or knitted fiber strands that form a more rounded wick than flat wicks. Pigments and fragrances do not easily clog up this wick. The wick is the preferred wick for beeswax candles. The wick is also more robust than flat wicks and is frequently used in taper and pillar candles.

Cored Wicks

Cored wicks are often used in pillar, votive, devotional, and jar candles. The wick has a core to keep the wick upright when the wax liquefies. Commonly, cotton, paper, zinc, or tin is used as a core. The core can run inside the wick or can be curled around the wick. Zink cored wicks are the most popular cored wicks used. Although they are used for all types of waxes, a larger wick is needed with vegetable waxes, as they do not burn as hot as other wicks.

HTP ***Wicks***

HTP wicks are very popular in soy and vegetable oil candles, but are used for all types of waxes. The wick is made from flat braided cotton fiber with paper fibers interwoven in the wick. The result is a wick that burns cleanly, and curls reliably into the flame for a self-trimming burn. The wick typically burns hotter than other wicks.

CD Wicks

CD wicks are very similar to HTP wicks in that they are flat braid cotton fibers. However. CD wicks have paper woven around the cotton fibers. The result is a wick that burns very hot and allows for excellent wax flow through the wick, while also providing rigidity. Although they are used in all waxes, they are very popular in soy and vegetable oil candles due to their rigidness and hotter burn.

Hemp Wicks

Hemp wicks can come in all the types mentioned before. However. Instead of cotton, hemp is used. The hemp is more rigid than cotton, as well as causes the wick to burn hotter. They are a good choice for soy or vegetable oil wax candles.

Wooden Wicks

Although a bit unconventional and not used that much in candles (used in incense sticks), wooden wicks are the most rigid wicks available. The wick is 100% self-trimming, and will not mushroom (form a knot).

Wax

Several different types of waxes have been used over the ages, with animal fat, or talon, being some of the oldest. Today, paraffin candles are the most commonly sold candles on the mass market, with talon and beeswax being popular waxes for homemade candles.

Fat / Lard / *Tallow Candles*

Tallow candles are some of the oldest candles in existence with people using them for thousands of years. Normally, pig fat is used. However. Any animal fat can be used to make lard. Depending on the animal fat used, tallow candles vary in their hardness, with deer, goat, and elk making the hardest candles. For softer fats such as sheep fat, alum, stearic acid, or beeswax is often added to the animal fat to make the wax harder.

Why Some Love It:

Tallow is easy to obtain and work with. It can be cheap if you use leftover fat from cooking, as well as not needing to worry about clogging up drainpipes when discarding leftover cooking fat. Some believe that tallow candles are more powerful than other candles, due to their belief that some of the energy of the animal is in the fat and adds to the spell. This is often utilized in curse magic.

Why Some Hate It:

It comes from animals. The smell is often not pleasant unless beeswax or fragrances are added to the candle. They do not burn as bright as paraffin candles and do not give off the warm glow of beeswax candles. Some say that tallow candles are only used by evil or satanic practitioners as it is derived from animal fat. This is a personal perception, as at one time in history, almost all churches used tallow candles before paraffin candles. And if you truly want to be technical, paraffin is from crude oil that is from dead animals and plants. Thus, if you really want to be pure, use soy or beeswax.

Beeswax Candles

Beeswax, like tallow candles, have been used for centuries. However. Due to their price, mostly the rich and churches could afford them. The oldest intact beeswax candles north of the Alps date from the 6th/7th century AD, and were found in the Alamannic graveyard of Oberflacht, Germany. From an experiment in 1946, it was found that around six to eight pounds of honey produce around one pound of wax. A typical beehive produces on average 30 pounds of honey.

Why Some Love It:
It comes directly from nature. The candles have a very pleasant smell and release negative ions that improve the mood in a room as well as help with pollution. The candles burn with a warm glow. Beeswax candles are a favorite in healing and prosperity spells as the wax is seen as pure and good. Beeswax is harder than tallow and does not require the addition of chemicals to be used. The wax is easy to use and reasonably easy to obtain. Beeswax is very easy to work with. It can be melted and poured into candle molds, or rolled into a candle by using beeswax sheets.

Why Some Hate It:
Beeswax is expensive, around ten times that of paraffin candles.
However. Beeswax is the preferred wax for home candle-making enthusiasts.

Paraffin Candles

Paraffin candles were introduced to the mass market in the early 1850s. Being almost ten times cheaper than most other waxes, it is now the most popular candle wax available. Paraffin is the final byproduct in petroleum refining, and burns clear with less smell than tallow candles. However. It is too soft to be used as is, and alum or stearic acid needs to be added to the wax.

Why Some Love It:
They are cheap to buy and available at many stores, in a variety of shapes and colors. Mass market candles burn reliably. It burns clean with little or no smell. Being soft, they are easy to engrave (writing the spell on the candle).

Why Some Hate It:
The big concern for paraffin candles is the toxic chemicals often added to the wax as well as that the wax is bleached. However. Bleach is sometimes added to soy wax as well.

Some of the chemicals that may be found in paraffin candles are Benzene, Toluene, Acetone, Trichlorofluoromethane, Carbon Disulfide, 2-Butanone, Trichloroethane, Trichloroethene, Carbon Tetrachloride, Tetrachloroethene, Chlorobenzene, Ethylbenzene, Styrene, Xylene, Phenol, Cresol, and Cyclopentene. Many of which are toxic and found in paint, lacquer, and varnish removers. Others are carcinogenic. However. The amount released from a candle cannot be compared to that of a diesel truck or even a back yard barbeque fire (many firelighters, and some briquettes contain paraffin).

Soy ***Wax Candles***

Soy wax is created from the soybean and is said to be a more sustainable source than paraffin wax. It was discovered in 1991 as an alternative to paraffin wax. Although more expensive than paraffin candles, they are a favorite among people that want to burn natural candles. Soy wax has a lower melting point than paraffin candles and tends to be softer than paraffin candles. Soy candles normally burn longer than paraffin candles, and cooler.

Why Some Love It:
Thought to be all-natural, renewable, non-toxic, and biodegradable. It burns longer and cooler than paraffin candles.

Why Some Hate It:
Soy candles are, in fact, not all-natural. To get soy wax, the soybean oil first needs to be chemically bleached to remove color and aroma. Normally, 100% bleach is used. The bleached oil is then hydrogenated with nickel (a heavy metal), to convert it into a solid wax. Thus, soy wax is in essence chemically bleached, heavy metal hydrogenated oil. Only pure beeswax is natural.

Perfumes

Many of the scented candles contain a combination of natural and synthetic fragrances. However. Cheap candles may only contain synthetic fragrances. Since synthetic fragrances add no additional power to the spell compared to natural fragrances or oils, it is better to buy unscented candles and anoint them with oil when doing magic.

Each fragrance oil (essential) comes from a different plant and has a different flashpoint. Some oils such as musk, vanilla, and amber do not travel up a wick as easily and can clog the wick. When using oils like these, a larger wick is required. If not, the flame may burn low or even die. Alternatively, the oil may clog the wick and form a mushroom (knot).

Know that citrus fragrances burn easier and adding too much to a candle can cause it to spontaneously combust. Alternatively, too much oil can travel up the wick, causing the citrus fragrance to give off a petroleum aroma instead of a citrus aroma.

Coloring

Color is an important aspect of spell casting, and the second-most important factor (after fragrance) for influencing consumer-purchasing decisions for household use.

There are two ways to color a candle, by using dyes or pigments.

Dyes

Dyes are available in liquid or powder form. They are easily combustible, will not clog a wick, and generally have little effect on the burning of a candle. Dyes are used to color a candle throughout, and can be mixed in a variety of shades. It has a slightly translucent look.

Pigments

Pigments are used to color the outside of a candle and are microscopic, suspended color particles that create a solid color, much like paint. The pigment will not easily bleed off like dye, but does not burn well and may clog the wick. Pigment is more used for decoration candles where only the outside is colored, such as silver or gold display candles.

A Note on Burning Candles

There are a lot of opinions around burning candles, especially paraffin candles, with the emphasis on using soy or beeswax candles. The truth is that, regardless of the wax used, all candle waxes are essentially carbon based, and when used, give off heat, light, water vapor (H_2O), molecular carbon (C), hydrocarbon (CH), and carbon dioxide (CO_2). Basically much of what we exhale.

Furthermore, note that, if the candle does not burn correctly, any candle can release soot that may be harmful to you. The smoke or soot from a candle is far less than that from a barbeque or a diesel truck smoking, and just as you should not stand by a barbeque fire or the exhaust of a running vehicle and inhale the fumes, so should you not inhale the smoke from a burning candle.

Chapter 5: The Science Behind The Light

For many people, the mystical flame holds them spellbound, without them knowing how the flame came to be. Although practically simple, there is a lot of chemistry and physics behind a candle flame. This has led even scientists from NASA to study candle flame behavior in microgravity with space shuttle experiments.

At its most simple, a burning candle consists of a fuel (normally a wax that is essentially hydrocarbons), a wick serving as a delivery method, and a flame, commonly called a diffusion flame. When a candle burns, the heat from the flame melts the wax near the wick where the temperature is around 600 degrees °C (1112 degrees °F). The heat causes the carbon and hydrogen atoms to break apart, and combine with oxygen to form a gas (called pyrolysis).

Due to capillary action (the attractive molecular forces between the wax molecules and the wick molecules pull the wax upward), the melted wax is drawn up the wick to the flame. There it is vaporized (turned into a hot gas) near the top of the wick, and the hydrocarbon molecules in the wax are broken down into hydrogen and carbon molecules. The flame here appears blue due to sufficient oxygen being provided for the reaction. The temperature is normally from 800 at the wick to around 1000 degrees °C (1472 - 1832 degrees °F) at the top of the blue zone. In the flame, the molecules react with oxygen from the surrounding air and create heat, light, water vapor (H2O), molecular carbon (C), hydrocarbon (CH), and carbon dioxide (CO2). The flame you see is the chemical reaction of carbon and hydrogen atoms with oxygen.

You will notice a small air gap between the flame and the wax. This is because solid wax does not burn, but first needs to be melted and vaporized. The blue zone may extend to the outside of the flame. The size of the blue zone depends on the diameter of the wick and the height of the flame, and may range from barely visible to nearly to the top of the yellow zone. The blue zone also called the reaction zone, gets its color primarily due to the chemical reaction where molecular carbon (C) and hydrocarbon (CH), or soot, are formed.

After the blue zone, is normally an orange-brown zone. This is where the luminous carbon region begins, and the temperature starts at around 1000 degrees °C (1832 degrees °F). There is relatively little oxygen in this zone. Various forms of carbon continue to break down, and small-hardened carbon particles start to form.

After the orange-brown zone, is the yellow zone or luminous carbon zone, which is responsible for most of the candle's light. In this zone, the carbon particles continue to heat up until they ignite and emit the full spectrum of visible light. The yellow portion of the spectrum is the most dominant, causing the flame to appear yellowish. As the carbon particles are consumed, carbon dioxide and water vapor are released (the same gasses we breathe out). The top of the yellow zone is around 1200 degrees °C (2192 degrees °F). Interestingly, the hottest part of the candle is the faint outside blue edge (sometimes called the veil), which extends from the blue zone at the base of the flame and up the sides of the yellow zone. The blue color is due to the flame having the highest concentration of oxygen at the edges. Typically, the temperature here is around 1400 degrees °C (2552 degrees °F).

As the candle burns, the flame heats the nearby air. The hot air rises up, causing a small vacuum below it. Cool air rises to replace the warm air, which in turn is heated as well. This causes a continual cycle of upward-moving air around the flame, called a convection current. This movement of air gives the flame its elongated or teardrop shape.

If the air to fuel (wax) ratio delivery is correct, the flame will settle into a steady-state with the classic teardrop form. Various factors influence the flame, and can cause it to from sputter and die out, to flare up and melt the candle away in record time. Most paraffin candles have stearin (stearic acid) added to them to raise the melting point of the candle. This allows the candle to burn slower. Too much stearic acid can cause the candle to fail to burn, and too little can cause the candle to melt away very fast. Normally, if the wax is too hard or mixed with too much color dye and additives, or the wick is too small, the flame will not be able to heat the top of the candle enough to supply the flame with enough fuel, causing the flame to die.

If the wax is too soft, the wick is too large or long, the flame may grow too large and melt the top of the candle too much. This will result in excess fuel being pulled up the wick, causing the flame to grow even larger. Eventually, carbon molecules (soot) will reach the top of the candle before they are consumed, causing the candle to smoke. The candle may melt away and waste most of the wax.

The candle may also smoke with a small flame if there is too little oxygen (typical of long glass candles), and eventually the flame may die out.

A flame that flickers can be a result of impurities in the candle wax, improper mixing of the wax and additives, an incorrect wick, moisture in the wick or wax, or air disturbance near the candle flame.

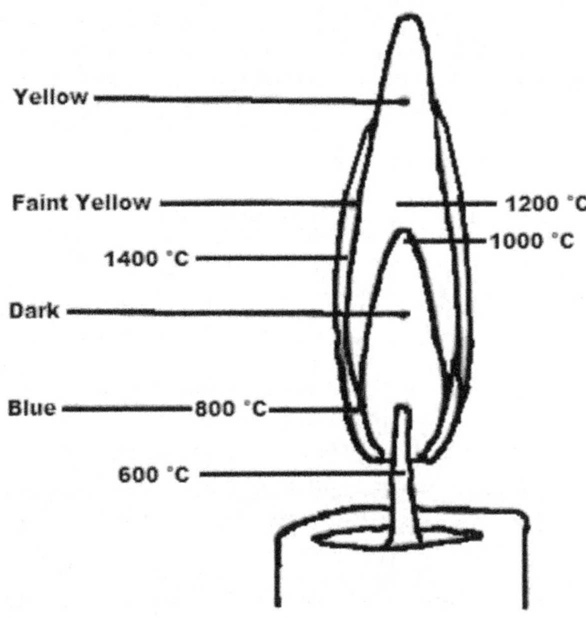

Chapter 6: Selecting the Right Candle

A candle is a candle, right? Not exactly. Although you can substitute several differently shaped and colored candles for almost any spell, there are times that for best results, you need to use a specific candle. Using an appropriate candle will help you visualize your desires and strengthen the spell. In all the candle groups, you may find scented and unscented candles. For the most part, unscented is better, as often the scents used in mass-market candles are not natural, but chemical. Even for handmade candles using true oils, scented candles limit their use and are only recommended if you buy them for a specific purpose. Even so, anointing a candle yourself with essential oils and herbs is often more powerful.

Bigger is better, right? Not always. Although yes, a bigger candle has potentially more energy than a smaller candle and will burn longer, it is not always needed or practical. Leaving a candle unattended is a fire risk.

The four-inch menorah candle sold in many stores is a popular candle used for spells. They burn reliably and are perfect for spell work. Another very popular candle for spell work, especially when traveling or when you have little space to work in, is a tea light candle.

The size of the candle normally depends on how fast you want the spell completed, as well as how much additional energy from the candle you need. The more discreet you need to be, the smaller the candle will need to be. For a quick spell or discreet workings, you may use a birthday cake candle or a tea light candle in the bathroom. Very large candles can add a lot of extra power to your spell, and some running a day or more (normally, glass-encased seven-day candles) are often used to break curses, obstacles, an opponent's defenses, and other spells.

Do know that with long spells, outside forces or an opponent may counter your spell before yours are done.

Always Use a New Candle

Never ever reuse a candle. A candle used to light the dinner table or bathroom cannot be used in a spell. And a candle that was used halfway for one spell cannot be used for another spell. Never break a candle in half to make two candles.

When a candle is used, even for a dinner setting, it picks up vibrations and energy, as well as your intent for its use. It gets charged with that intent, even if you did not focus your intent on it. Merely lighting a candle charges it to an extent for the purpose you are lighting it for.

If you reuse a candle, the vibrations and energy inside the candle may conflict with the new intent, and can lead to unwanted results. Some practitioners believe that the moment a candle is lit; it attracts negative vibrations from things around it. This is one reason they do not like to use large candles, purify the area before spell work, throw salt around the candleholders, and sometimes wrap the candle in foil. Foil is used to protect and amplify the spell's energy.

Candle Inspection

Regardless of the candle you use, always inspect it carefully before you buy it, and then again, before you use it. Candles are fragile, and may have cracks in or worse, be broken in half, from mishandling or incorrect molding. This will be disastrous to your spell and possibly you.

Other things to look out for are inconsistent color, normally due to the candlemaker not mixing the wax properly or running out of wax and then using a new batch to complete the candle molding. Always make sure that the wick is aligned with the center of the candle from top to bottom, especially on thick candles.

Although rare, I have found candles where the candle maker's hair ended up in a candle, as well as nail clippings and dirt. Expect your spell to possibly backfire disastrously if foreign items are in the candle when used.

On the left, a correct candle. In the middle, the wick is skew and the candle may burn only on one side. On the right, not only is the wick skew in the candle but there are two wicks. Always inspect your candle. These were hand-made candles I pulled from the shelf, of a local esoteric shop.

Standard Straight Candle

The standard straight candle is the most popular and versatile, with the color white good for almost anything in a pinch (even as a substitute for black). The candle may have decorations such as spirals or ribs on the side, but in essence, it is just a straight candle. The commercial candles available at most supermarkets burn very reliably, and are reasonably cheap. Do not use scented ones in your spells, as these often contain artificial scent and not real oils.

Notched Candles

A notched candle is about the only candle meant to be stopped and restarted. With this candle, a notch is burned each day. The candle is stopped after a notch is burned down, and then restarted the next day at the same time. This intensifies the power of your spell in the same manner as repeating the same spell multiple days with smaller candles. However. As you are only using one candle, you only need to anoint and charge one candle once, making it a bit easier.

These candles are not suggested for curse breaking, as some believe just as the spell gets momentum, you stop the spell and give the opposition time to retaliate and block your spell. They can work well for prosperity and business success spells, as well as love spells.

Glass Covered Candles

In some parts of the world, these are the most popular candles around, especially the seven-day candles. The glass holder is often covered in premade spells, such as love, curse breaker, prosperity, and money. Some may have devotions to deities or angels on them. With these premade candles, a practitioner need only say the words printed on the glass, and light the candle. The clear glass holder candles are very popular with hoodoo and voodoo practitioners in many parts of the world, as the candle burns very long, the flame is mostly protected from wind, and foil can be wrapped around the candle. When I lived in the Cayman Islands, this is the only candle I used. From the voodoo practitioners on the island, I was taught that wrapping foil around a candle amplifies the power of the spell, while also focusing the energy, as well as blinding any divination from another who is trying to see what spell you are doing. (A tea light candle does the same but just burns shorter.)

Figure Candles

Figure candles are more popular in love and curse magic, but can be used for healing magic. The belief is that when using a candle in the shape of a person, it is the same as making a voodoo doll and the candle now becomes part of the person the spell is aimed at. This takes the spell to a new level than just burning a normal candle. Red and pink figure candles in the shape of a man and woman are normally used in love spells. Black-figure candles in curses or to break a love relationship. Skull candles are normally used for mind games, confusing an opponent (often used in court cases), or to give a person clarity of mind or heal a mental illness. Figure candles in the shape of a dollar sign are often used in prosperity spells. Although more expensive than a normal candle, the addition of a figure candle can greatly help to focus your intent, and amplify your spell's power.

Container Candles

Container candles are mostly used in restaurants or religious places where long-burning candles that burn safely are required. However. Many are often only used as display candles. A container candle is any candle that is poured into a container (even glass), and intended to be burned. The benefit of container candles is that they can stand on their own, and often the flame is protected so that wind does not affect it much. Fire hazard is also kept to a minimum. Containers can be decorative, such as in the shape of an oil lamp. Popular ones are jar container candles. They burn very long, but are expensive.

Pillar Candles

Pillar candles are an upgrade from a standard straight candle, and are often several inches wide and tall. When I lived in South East Asia, I used candles over 1.5 meters high (almost 5 feet). The cross-section can be a circle, oval, or hexagon. The candles are often used in religious settings, as they burn long. However. Cheap pillar candles often have a too thin wick for the candle width. The flame often makes only a hollow in the wax for a few inches without melting the sides away. Eventually, the candle will die as not enough air gets to the wick. One then needs to keep cutting the leftover wax rim away (a soldering iron works best).

Do not use the pillar candles bought in normal supermarkets as they often burn as described above, and can cause your spell to fail miserably. If you want to use a pillar candle, get a quality one directly from a candle manufacturer and make sure the wick is thick enough to burn all the way to the sides of the candle. Apart from religious settings such as churches, pillar candles are used for very long and very powerful spells. However. It takes a lot of dedication to do the spell and is normally only used in high magic. Do note that because of the large amount of wax pillar candles have, if the wax runs, it can create a big mess. Never place a pillar candle directly on a delicate surface, and make sure that the candleholder can hold all the wax that may melt away.

Novelty Candles

Novelty candles are irregularly shaped candles (some in the shape of objects such as cars or Buddha or a person) and are made by molding, sculpting, and or pouring. They are not actually intended to be burned, but more for display. However. Some people do use them in curse magic, as in set someone's house or car on fire.

Taper Candles

Taper candles as the name suggests, go from large at the base, to normally a sharp point the size of the wick at the top. They are often used in romantic settings or at dinner tables. Some believe that taper candles work better than others do. But it is only a personal belief and partly due to a nostalgic memory as taper candles were used for a long time, as they are easier to get out of a mold. Some also believe that as there is less wax at the top, the candle will burn down faster in the beginning, and as such, the spell will start faster. If you believe this and want a fast candle, use a birthday cake candle. In the end, it is your belief that counts.

Votive and Tea Lights

These candles originated in churches, but nowadays more refer to any small plug-type candle that is around 1 1/2 inches in diameter and around 2 to 3 inches high. Tea light candles are one of the most popular candles for small spaces, especially bathrooms. The larger size votive candles are normally used for catering to hold food warm. Tea light candles are a good option for travel, when you have little space, have a short spell, or need to be discreet.

Most tea light candles can easily be removed from the metal holder, anointed with oil, engraved (symbols edged into them), and then replaced. No one will even know the candle you put on the dinner table or even in the living room when there are guests, is a spell. Tea light candles also do not run, and normally do not make a mess. However. The metal holder does get hot, so always place the candles on a heatproof surface.

As mentioned before, the metal around the tea light creates a protective barrier against influences as well as divination, and amplifies your spell the same as wrapping it in foil or placing a mirror under the candle. In Feng Shui, a mirror amplifies what it reflects. This principle is used in magic by amplifying the energy of the spell. Wrapping foil around a candle is also believed to capture any energy going to the sides, and focusing it upwards. This is believed to create a laser focus spell that cuts through any obstacles. Using a curved mirror under a candle can have the same effect by focusing the energy. Almost like a satellite dish. I like using the curved mirrors that magnify things 10 times, often found in shops by the makeup section.

Note. Do not wrap foil around a long thin candle that is not encased in glass. The flame on a thin unprotected candle is too close to the foil and can cause the foil to burn. The candle will also heat up too much and melt away very fast.

Chapter 7: Guidelines to Practicing Candle Magic

Candle magic is as simple or complex, as you desire. Remember, intent and visualization are key. Following are some steps to help you start if you are new to candle magic.

Step One: Do You Really Need a Spell?

Before you rush out to the local magic store to get supplies, first think about what you actually desire and need. You may not even need a spell. For instance, you may think you need a fortune spell to help with your finances, where what you need is a new job spell or just stopping in buying a new outfit every weekend. You may also think you need a love spell to make a person fall in love with you, where what you may need is a self-love spell so that you take better care of yourself and become a more likable person. You may also want revenge for the person that placed a spell on you and are thinking about a reverse spell, but if you are just starting out, an uncrossing spell is a far better option. It is also no use in doing a get a job or prosperity spell when the bills are due the next day. A better option would be a compassion spell where people will give you an extension on paying your bills. It is also useless in doing a justice spell in your favor, when the case may be postponed or people are still giving testimony. Often, a judge only gives his or her verdict a week or two after all the witnesses testified.

You can ask your local magic shop or coven to help you with a spell for your situation, or you can look at the back of the book for ideas. As a new practitioner, be careful of using spells found online. Often, people post spells without informing you of the consequences (especially when using deities). Never do a spell involving any deity that you do not know and are comfortable in working with. Or say words in a langue you do not know.

Step Two: Get the Ingredients

For first-time practitioners, I recommend buying ready-made spell kits. You even get single pre-charged candles for a specific purpose, such as house protection, banishing, money, and so on.

Spell kits make sourcing the ingredients very easy, as well as that most kits are intended for first-time practitioners, and normally have easy-to-follow instructions in the kit.

Another benefit of spell kits is, that you now have a spell with full instructions that you can add to your spellbook for later use. With pre-charged spells, you are also piggybacking on the power of the person who charged the candles, enhancing the chances of success of the spell. If you grow your own herbs or make your own candles, you will now be gathering the herbs needed or mold your candle/s specific to your spell. This adds great power to the spell, but requires more time and effort.

Step Three: Cleanse Yourself

You may be overjoyed with doing your spell, but remember, you need to cleanse yourself from the day's dirt and sweat, as well as any negativity that may be clinging to you from other people you met during the day. Taking a bath with a spoonful of coarse salt and three drops of rosemary (or rose) oil is a good way to start. If you have no coarse salt or rosemary oil, use a small packet or tablespoon full of Epson salt. At the very least, add a spoon full of normal table salt to your bathwater, or washcloth if you take a shower. You can also add a teaspoon of dried rosemary herbs to your bath water from the spice rack if you do not have the oil.

Step Four: Cleanse Your Environment

Negativity naturally accumulates in an area, especially if there is fighting in a house, you stress a lot, as well as if you have negative thoughts. Power-hungry entities that feed off your power as you practice magic also accumulate and can sap the power of spells. Negative sex (any sex where both partners are not doing it out of love, as well as masturbation) can lend energy to negative entities as at climax immense energy is released without direction. With normal sex where love is involved, the energy is transferred to the partner. Depending on what protection you have around your house or area of practice, you may have many entities that could cause your spells to fail.

A good way to cleanse an area before a spell is to burn a White Sage incense stick just before starting your spell, possibly even while you take a bath. If you have no white sage or cannot burn anything, then a pinch of salt, even table salt, thrown around the room will do. Remember, it is about the intention so no need to cover the floor in salt. At the very least, white light the room by imagining a white light filling the room and causing all evil to flee or evaporate.

Step Five: Cast a Protection Circle

This can be as easy as closing your eyes for a moment and imagining a ring of energy of white or blue protecting you, to as elaborate as actually making a circle with salt and other objects. It does not matter, as intent is the key. What matters is that you protect yourself. It is believed that negative entities cannot enter the circle and attack you while you are busy with the spell, nor affect the spell. Remember to take the circle down after you are done with the spell else it may drain your energy.

Crushed herbs with protective properties mixed with salt make an excellent tool to block negative influences. Alternatively, you can burn protective herbs on a charcoal block, oil in an oil diffuser, or use scented incense to clear your space and protect it. Good choices are white sage, sandalwood, frankincense, dragon's blood, and lavender.

Step Six: Prepare Your Area

If you have an altar, you would now prepare your altar by placing the items that you want and need for the spell on your altar. Place the candleholders for the altar and spell candles in the positions that you want then, with the candles either in the holders or in front of them, ready to be prepared. I like placing the candles in front of the holders so that I can visually see a candle still needs preparation less I possibly forget to prepare a candle.

Step Seven: Cleanse Your Candle/s and Ingredients

Always cleanse candles you bought that are not part of a spell kit or pre-charged for a specific spell. You never know who handled the candle before you. Often, negativity clings to people or follows them, and some of the negativity may have attached to the candle when the people handled the candle before you.

Take a paper tissue and wet it lightly with non-scented rubbing alcohol (can be bought from most chemists /drug stores). Gently clean the surface of the candle from the bottom up while imagining all negativity being pulled out of the candle.

With encased candles, clean the exposed wax as well as the holder. Lastly, gently wipe the wick. For herbs and incense sticks or cones, hold your dominant hand over them, and then imagine pulling out the negativity from them and throwing it away. You can use the same method for candles if you have no rubbing alcohol or have pre-prepared candles.

Before laughing at cleaning a candle before use, think about this for a moment. You do not know what the people handled before handling the candle and placing it back, which you may have bought. The rubbing alcohol will remove fingerprints and the oil naturally found on people's hands, from the candle. If a person's hands were very sweaty, or they ate a greasy meal (like a cheeseburger), or worse used the toilet (loo) and did not wash their hands before handling the candle, that oil and crap are on the candle and can ruin your spell if not removed. Lastly, remember that candles can be programmed for an intent. How do you know that a resentful or evil-minded person did not pick up the candle before you and programmed it to fail for any spell it was used for by any other person but them? A person may know an opponent is buying their candles at a certain store and may go there and curse or hex all the candles in the store in the hope to ruin the opposition, without caring what happens to other practitioners. If there were no evil practitioners, we would not need uncrossing and hex-breaking spells.

Remember to cut the exposed wick to around ¼ inch in length to prevent it from creating a large flame that will possibly melt the candle away and cause it to smoke.

Step Eight: Consecrate the Candle

When you consecrate the candle, you are dedicating it to your intended purpose. Candles from spell kits or pre-charged candles are already consecrated.

How you consecrate the candle, is up to you. You can simply hold each candle in your hands and visualize what the candle's purpose is, or you can go further and carve sigils, symbols, or runes into the candle with a knife, toothpick, needle, or so on. You can even write the spell on the candle if you wish.

For a long spell, start from the top and write in a spiral all around the candle to the bottom (in the same direction you would oil the candle). While doing this, think hard on your spell and see it working successfully with no obstacles. It does happen that obstacles, blockages, or resistance are seen at this point while trying to envision the spell. Fight them off in any way you want and focus your intention and imagination towards the spell and a successful outcome.

For added effect, just like writing a spell on paper, write your words in the candle with a colored ink pen that corresponds to the spell you are doing. Alternatively, first, trace the words or symbols in the candle with a needle or sharp object, then retrace them with a cotton bud dipped in dragon's blood ink for general spells and protection, patchouli for money, doves' blood ink for love, and war water or four thieves vinegar for banishing and curse-breaking.

If you do not have four fingers vinegar, you can use white vinegar, and if you do not have war water, you can edge the symbols and words in the candle with a rusty nail or piece of rusty iron. Never use these for spells other than hex and curse breaking, protection, or banishing spells. Iron is seen as the menstrual blood of the earth and is one of the strongest magical items around. It gives your spells power while drawing negative energy away from you as well as weakening your enemy.

Step Nine: Write the Spell If Desired

If you like to write the spell or petition down on paper, do so now. You can use colored paper or plain white. Often, parchment paper is used, but anything is okay. However. Lined paper is seen as either too rigid not allowing the universe to give you part of the spell, while some see it as the possibility that the universe may 'read between the lines' and give you something you did not ask for.

To be on the safe side either way, use unlined paper if you can. Never use blocked paper, as this is seen as crossing out your spell.

Step Ten: Anoint the Candle

Although it is true that you do not absolutely need to anoint a candle, the oil can aid in the success of the spell, especially if you use oil made specifically for the spell, such as prosperity or uncrossing and so on oil. If you are starting out, buy ready-made oil from your local magic shop. If you do not like oil, you can use scented water that was made for a specific purpose. Such as Florida water for cleansing, war water, or four fingers vinegar water for protection and possibly banishing. Holy water can be used for either protection or banishing of evil and rosewater for love and cleansing.

If you cannot find a specific oil for your spell, you can use olive or almond oil. Intent is key. Remember that if you use purpose-made oil or water, it can only be used on the candle (or part of it) that corresponds to that oil. Thus, a spell with a black and white candle for uncrossing and return of funds would use uncrossing oil on the black candle and prosperity oil on the white candle (or parts of a twin color candle). The exception is an oil that both repels negativity as well as attracts good, such as van van oil, crown of success, and High John the Conquer.

Anointing the candle is not just adding extra power (the oil) to the spell, but is seen as establishing a psychic link between the candle and you. The candle now becomes an extension of you through a sensory experience. You are now charging the candle with your own personal vibrations as well as programming the desired spell or petition into the candle.

The direction you anoint a candle is an ongoing debate, with each person deciding on his or her own method. Here are the more commonly accepted ways to do it. Experiment, and decide what works for you, again, intent and imagination are key.

For encased candles, such as glass-encased candles, you can gently oil the glass, as you would have done with a normal candle. As the candle burns, the oil will be heated and give off its scent. Additionally, anoint the exposed part of the wax if you want. Normally, for a remove or banish spell, anoint counter-clockwise (widdershins) around the wick and to attract something, anoint clockwise (deosil) around the wick. Remember that tea light candles can often be removed from the metal holder, anointed, and then replaced.

Single Candle Single Purpose

Method One: To remove or banish something, rub from the bottom of the candle to the top of the candle. To attract something, rub from the top of the candle to the bottom. Hold the bottom of the candle towards you so that when you rub up, you rub away from you and when you rub down the candle, you rub towards you.

Method Two: To remove or banish something, rub oil from the middle of the candle outwards towards the top and bottom of the candle respectively. To attract something, rub oil from the top and bottom of the candle towards the center of the candle.

Method Three: To remove or banish something, rub oil counter-clockwise (widdershins) around the candle. To attract something, rub oil clockwise (deosil) around the candle. This method works very well with small candles, especially tea light candles.

Method Four: Combine methods one and three. Thus, to remove or banish something, rub from the bottom of the candle, counter-clockwise (widdershins) around the candle in a spiral, to the top of the candle. To attract something, rub from the top of the candle, clockwise (deosil) around the candle in a spiral, to the bottom. Hold the bottom of the candle towards you so that when you rub up, you rub away from you and when you rub down the candle, you rub towards you.

Method Five: Combine methods two and three. Thus, to remove or banish something, rub oil from the middle of the candle, counter-clockwise (widdershins) around the candle in a spiral, outwards towards the top and bottom of the candle respectively. To attract something, rub oil from the top and bottom of the candle, clockwise (deosil) around the candle in a spiral, towards the center of the candle.

Single Candle Dual Purpose With Different Directions

Using a candle for two different purposes has been popular since ancient times due to the scarcity of candles. This gave rise to the popularity of many practitioners to anoint the candle from the center outwards as many spells were done to banish or ward off evil and then restore what was lost.

Nowadays, dual-purpose candles are often found in reversing or banishing spells, where the top half is normally black, and the bottom half is normally white or red. If you cannot find a dual-color candle and need one for a spell, use two different candles with the colors you need, or a single white (or your choice of color) candle and anoint the halves as if they were the colors you need. Personally, I would not use a single-color candle for a dual candle spell, especially a black candle. Using black for attraction may create unwanted results. However. You can split any candle in two with imagination and give each part a different purpose.

Note, with duel spell candles, the top half of the candle is normally to remove or banish something, and the bottom part is to attract something. If the candle halves are reversed in their purpose, as in, the top half is to attract something and the bottom half of the candle is to banish something, which is uncommon, reverse the anointing order given below. However. The black or banishing part should be on top as you first want to banish something from your life, such as a person, poverty, or a hex, and then want to attract back what you lost.

Method One: Anoint from the middle of the candle outwards towards the top and bottom of the candle respectively.

Method Two: Anoint the top half, counter-clockwise (widdershins) around the candle. Then, anoint the lower half, clockwise (deosil) around the candle.

Method Three: Combine methods one and two. Anoint from the middle of the candle, counter-clockwise (widdershins) around the candle in a spiral, to the top of the candle. Then, anoint from the middle of the candle, clockwise (deosil) around the candle in a spiral, to the bottom of the candle.

Single Candle Dual Purpose of the Same Direction

This is an uncommon method, and normally used when the candle halves have two different purposes, yet the same direction, as in either banish or attract.

Say you want to attract both a new position at your work and a pay raise. You could do it with a single spell or two spells. However. You may want to combine the two spells because you may not want the pay raise without the new position nor the new position without the pay raise. Splitting the candle in two allows you to see how the flame burns for each request while using only one candle.

Method One: For attraction, anoint from the top to the middle of the candle while imagining that half of the candle for one request, then anoint from the middle of the candle to the bottom of the candle for the second attraction request. For banishing, anoint from the middle of the candle upwards for one request, and then from the bottom of the candle to the middle for the second request.

Method Two: For attraction, anoint the top half, clockwise (deosil) around the candle. Then, anoint the lower half, clockwise (deosil) around the candle. For banishing, anoint the top half, counter-clockwise (widdershins) around the candle. Then, anoint the lower half, counter-clockwise (widdershins) around the candle.

Method Three: Combining methods one and two. For attraction, anoint from the top to the middle of the candle, clockwise (deosil) in a spiral around the candle, while imagining that half of the candle for one request, then anoint from the middle of the candle to the bottom of the candle, clockwise (deosil) around the candle in a spiral, for the second attraction request. For banishing, anoint from the middle of the candle upwards, counter-clockwise (widdershins) around the candle in a spiral for one request, and then from the bottom of the candle to the middle of the candle, counter-clockwise (widdershins) around the candle in a spiral, for the second request.

Anoint the Wick

Do not forget to anoint the wick. The method you use to anoint the wick will largely depend on how you anointed the candle, and if it is for a single or dual-purpose spell.

Method One: If the candle is used for a single purpose, then anoint the wick clockwise (deosil) to attract something, and counter-clockwise (widdershins) to banish or expel something.
Method Two: If the candle is used for a single purpose, then anoint the wick upwards for banishing and downwards for attraction, at the same time you anoint the candle.

Method Three: If the candle is for a dual purpose, then anoint the wick at the same time you are doing the top half, in the same manner, and with the same oil, as this is how the candle will start.

Method Four: If the candle is for a dual purpose, then anoint the wick at the same time you are doing the top half, in the same manner, but with a neutral oil. This is if you feel you do not want to have the wick that is the center of the candle, dedicated with say banishing oil, when the bottom half of the candle uses prosperity oil for attraction.

Step Eleven: Add Herbs

Lastly, add (normally sprinkle) any herbs or powders you want onto the candle. You can roll the candle in herbs, but be careful not to add too much, and watch the direction you are rolling the candle.

This method is only recommended if the candle is for a single purpose. Else, sprinkle herbs on the candle on each part of the candle in the same way you applied the oil to that part of the candle. Do not add herbs or powder to the top of the candle, as it may clog the wick and cause the flame to fade or die.

For added effect, use an oil diffuser (the kind that takes a tea light in the bottom with oil in a holder) and place the same oil you are using for your candle in it. If you are using a double candle, such as for reversing, use van van oil. If you do not have an oil diffuser or do not want to use oil, you can use granules in water in the diffuser or use incense sticks and cones. Note that incense sticks last longer than cones, but make more of a mess.

Step Twelve: Charge the Candle

After Consecrating the candle to a specific purpose, add power to the candle by either holding it in your hands or holding your hands around the candle, an inch away. Imagine power streaming from your hands towards the candle.

You can pull power from your surroundings, the moon, the sun, or wherever you want, to add power to your spell. Some do this before or while they are anointing the candle, this is up to you. What is important is that you are happy with how you conduct your spell. At this point, you would place the candle in its holder, and if you wrote the spell on paper and wish to place it under the candle, do so now. Some practitioners place the paper directly under the candle in the holder, while others use glass-encased candles, and wrap the paper around the candle.

Step Thirteen: Light the Candle

There is a lot of discussion on whether you should use matches, a gas lighter, a paraffin lighter or lamp, or some other way of lighting the candle. For me, it is a personal thing, so use what you want. Following is why some people use or do not use a specific method.

Matches

Some practitioners believe in only using matches to light candles as they see the wood in the matches as a link to earth. However. Matches use sulfur that is seen as brimstone that is a banishing ingredient. Some practitioners believe that the smell may attract the devil or evil and that the sulfur is unclean. Others believe that the sulfur will lessen the power of a spell or render a spell useless, especially if it is for prosperity or protection as the sulfur is seen to banish the spell. However. Some practitioners explicitly use matches to light banishing and reversing spell candles because of the sulfur. Additionally, by lighting a match to start a candle, you add to the sulfur pollution in the air.

However. All said, the actual amount of sulfur in the match is very little, and to believe that burning that amount can call demons forth without the intention to call demons is a little absurd. It takes more than lighting a match to call a demon forth. If it did work, smokers and people lighting dinner candles would have scores of demons floating around them, not to mention the nuns and priests in churches.

Electric or Flint Activated Gas Lighters

Today, this type of lighter is the most versatile and used lighter in existence. They are cheap, safe, and reasonably reliable. Some are even refillable. The best ones to use are those that have an extended tube with the flame away from you and an electric trigger. Lighting several candles with a normal flint lighter can cause the flint wheel to heat up, possibly burning you. Some practitioners see this as too modern and not pure when doing magic. However. They have no problem using paraffin candles.

Electric or Flint Activated Paraffin Lighters and Lamps

This type of lighter is still hugely popular, especially the famed Zippo lighter that uses a flint and lighter fluid that is essentially paraffin. The lighters are normally robust and reliable. However. Some see them as possibly tainting the spell with their oil (paraffin) as it is unclean, which is funny as most commercial candles today are paraffin wax candles that although different paraffin, still comes from crude oil that originally comes from dead plants and animals.

Practitioners also fear the possibility of jinxing the spell if the lighter smokes (normally due to bad fuel being used or incorrectly adjusted flint).

Lighting Multiple Candles

If you have multiple candles with the same spell, such as a banishing and attraction spell with a black and white candle, then you would normally first light the black candle (banishing), then when the candle is almost used up, light the white (attraction candle) with the flame of the black candle. If you have any altar or protection candles, light them first, then light the spell's candles.

Step Fourteen: Burn the Candle

I personally do not like stopping a candle from burning, especially if it is a banishing or protection candle. I see a reversing, banishing, and uncrossing candle as going to war. For you are effectively trying to break someone else's negativity over you. If you stop the candle before it is done, it is like attacking another force in war, just to pull back before you attain victory. However. It is up to you how you want to burn your candles.

You can either burn the candle totally down, or burn only a specific portion or allotted time each day. The time the candle takes to burn depends on the size of the candle, as well as how the flame burns. A large candle is often seen as having the capacity to store more energy when you charge it as well as giving off more of its own energy, but it takes longer to complete and may give other practitioners time to counter your spell, choose wisely. Often it is better to do multiple smaller candles each day than a single large candle that burns for seven days. If you do multiple candles over multiple days for the same spell, you can save time by consecrating and anointing them all at the same time.

Stopping a Candle

If you have to stop a candle, use a candlesnuffer to do so. This does not damage the wick and allows you to stop the candle without causing smoke. Blowing out a candle is seen as blowing your spell away, even if you wave it out with your hand or another object to create air.

Pinching the candle flame dead is seen as pinching your spell dead. Of course, be careful if a person that wishes you ill should be in your place while you have a spell running. They may just blow or pinch your candle flames out. This goes for children and other guests as well that may stop your spells without thinking.

Step Fifteen: Clean Up

So, when is a spell done? Many believe when the flame is dead, but this is not so. The spell runs until all the energy is used up, whether the spell was successful or not. While the leftover wax or even candleholder is still on the area you burned the candle, the spell is still puling power from you. Many practitioners leave a spell candle for days or even weeks to gain additional energy before removing the items. As the circle you cast is for protection, you should decide when to take it down. Normally, it is after you cleaned up. However. For a spell running days, you may want to take it down after lighting the candle to spare your energy. However. You may run the risk of leaving the spell unprotected. In this case, it is a good idea to make a thin salt circle around the candleholder to keep negativity away.

The spell is done when you have disposed of the leftover wax, wick, and cleaned the altar of other props used for the spell. Most wax, including paraffin wax, is biodegradable. You can bury the wax, or throw it into running water. If you have no place to bury it and need to, for instance, you did a spell to gain something, then as a last resort, you can wrap the wax up in a brown paper bag and place the leftover wax under your bed.

Never place the leftover wax in a plastic bag, as it may block the energy from the spell, as to using foil. If you discard your leftover wax in your trash, you are treating your spells as trash, and eventually, it will end up on a landfill, where a lot of negative energy resides, not the place you want your prosperity spell wax to end up at. However. If you decide to recycle the wax, dispose of it in a recycling location while imagining the energy you put into the candle being recycled into the universe.

Normally, burying the wax is seen as creating a link with earth, and grounding the energy, allowing it to work. The same happens when letting it go in a river.

Take note that, candle magic is of nature, thus to release the energy back to nature finishes your spell. To put it another way. Doing candle magic is creating a link between the candle wax and the person, business, or situation you targeted, with the message you programmed into the wax. For instance, if you did a hex-breaking spell on yourself, the wax (or leftover wick), is a link to you, with the intention of removing all negativity from and around you. Burying the wax in the ground, lets the negativity from you flow into earth. Throwing it into running water lets the water clean the negativity from you.

In short, normally anything positive for yourself or another, you ideally want to bury close to you or the person, simulating planting a tree; that earth will nurture and let grow. Anything bad that you want away from you, you ideally want to throw in running water away from your house, and let the water cleanse you. For curses or hex-breaking, you may want to bury the items so that the person or situation rots as things that are dead do when buried. For love spells, you may want to throw the wax into water to have the water deliver the spell. Remember to always have respect for the leftover items.

Following are some suggestions for discarding the leftover wax and glass if using a glass-encased candle. You may need to improvise if you have no access to these places.

Important. For any curse, take a different path home and do not look back as you leave. In addition, avoid the road or place for at least three days.

Bury In the Backyard

The backyard is good for maintaining a situation, your finances, your possessions, your position in a company, and keeping a person in your life. This is due to the backyard being seen as where you keep your possessions, often things you do not want others to steal. Spells often done are marriage, prosperity, protection, and family harmony.

Bury In the Front Yard

Your front yard is where people arrive, and is good for attracting new opportunities, people, situations (travel and adventure), new jobs or work, and change into your life. This is due to the front yard normally being the place where you welcome arrivals to your house. Spells often buried here include, love, travel, health, marriage proposal, and job-seeking spells.

Bury In a Cemetery

A cemetery is seen as a final stop, endings, and letting go. However. It is also seen as a place of sorrow. For this reason, curse, banishing, remove obstacles, and hex-breaking spells are normally buried here. However. If you do not want to go into a cemetery, bury the items away from your home, possibly under (near) a large tree.

If you do bury items in a cemetery, always be respectful of the dead, and leave a few coins or candy at the gate when you leave.

Bury In the Target's Yard or Property

This will take some guts, and access to the property. However. I have hidden items in people's homes, with great results. Good places they will never find it, is behind wall sockets and light switches. You will have to remove the cover and watch out for the electricity. These are dire cases, but it works exceptionally well.

As you are burying it in the target's property, much the same goes for if you do it for yourself. Thus, any spell for the target can be buried in their yard or placed in their property (even business). Sometimes it will be with the approval of the target, such as a health or prosperity spell, and at other times, it may be against their knowledge such as a binding spell.

At the Target's Front Door Or In the Driveway

This way sends a visual message and is very bold, for the target may take drastic action. However. This may be exactly what you want. For you can place items (such as a small coffin with their picture in) by their front door, without doing a spell.

The target may then expend a lot of energy trying to break the death curse, and see everyday events as the curse, thereby cursing themselves, without you actually doing a curse. If the above reaction is not your intention, and you actually did a spell, then the items need to be inconspicuous. You could use oil, water (war water), or the leftover ash from an herb burning as well as powders. Do mix it with a bit of dirt so that it does not look too obvious.

Bury at a Business

Most often, this will be for your business or a client's business for prosperity or protection spells. If you cannot bury it in the yard, consider a pot plant by the front door. Cursing spells on the business or employees are also buried here. For any spell, make sure the items are discretely buried, and none of the employees sees you, even if the spell is for good. Some employees may go and dig the items up in revenge towards their boss.

Releasing Items Into Natural Water

Water is seen as cleansing and taking things away. Thus any flowing river, natural lake, ocean, or flowing stream will do. Do not use stagnant ponds, dams, reservoirs, or lakes. If there is no natural in and outflow, energy will stagnate, only use natural flowing water. The wax from any spell can be discarded in water. Streams are often used for love and cleansing spells. Oceans and rivers that are stronger are often used for banishing, curse and hex-breaking spells. Lakes are good for prosperity, health, binding, and career spells. If the company or person is overseas, a river leading to an ocean or the ocean is ideal.

The only exception for stagnant water, being ponds, swamps, and marches, is when doing curses or binding spells, and you live far from it. ***Never throw cursed items or leftover wax in water near your home or business.*** Regardless if it is a natural stream, river, or natural lake, if the water is part of a protected wildlife reserve, do not use it for cursing.

Active Train Tracks

Active train tracts are much the same as flowing water. Trains take things away, and deliver things. Thus, love, binding, manipulation, and curse spells can be delivered, and negativity can be taken away in banishing or hex-breaking spells. Be very careful, as trains will not stop for you.

Abandoned Train Tracks

Abandoned train tracks are used for banishing, separation, break-up, and letting go spells.

At an Intersection

An intersection can be either a four-way crossing, or a three-way (T-junction). Normally, binding spells are done at T-junctions, and curses, banishment, releasing, love, and commanding spells are done at four-way crossings. The T-junction stops the flow if you approach it from the road leading into the T-junction. Thus, it is used for binding spells. Four-way crossings go in all directions. It is used to deliver curses or spells to a person you do not know, or know where they stay. It can also be used for attracting prosperity from all directions.

Be very careful, for cars can run you over if you climb out, especially by night, and police may fine you for littering. A friend of mine was caught and had to explain at length why she dropped stuff in the road. I normally go late at night and then go to a busy intersection where there is a traffic light. I then slowly approach and wait just until the light turns green, then go for the intersection slowly. With my driver's window open, I slowly pass through the intersection and discreetly drop the items by hanging my arm out next to the door. In saying that, I do not discard leftover wax in a road, only lemon banishing and uncrossing spells. For prosperity spells, do not put stuff in the road, as cars will drive over your prosperity. Bury it next to the road if you cannot bury it at your place of business or you have an online business.

Leaving It In the Road

A direct road is seen the same as a train track, and used to deliver a love spell, curse, or controlling spell, or to take negativity away. Use a road that leads to the target's house or business for a curse or love spell.

I use this method for separation and banishing spells using a charcoal block. I would stop alongside a deserted road at night with the car running, then open my door slightly and place the charcoal block and powder or herbs next to the road. I then quickly light the charcoal while saying my incantation, then drive away as soon as I see the herbs smoldering.

Make sure to use a good quality charcoal brand that lights easily and does not die halfway through. You can add a bit of paraffin lighter fluid to old charcoal blocks. Remember not to look back.

Scattering Ashes To the Wind

This option is only for ashes from paper, or if only the ash from a wick remained. Any spell can be released this way, as you are giving the spell to air. With love, curse, binding, and controlling spells, the air will deliver the spell. For prosperity, healing, and protection spells, the air will blow life into the spell and deliver it to the universe.

Burning It

Fire destroys, and as such, never use it to discard any leftover wax from positive spells. Fire is used for curses, controlling spells, banishing, hex-breaking, release, breakups, separation, and so on. Remember the wax is a link to the situation, and the fire will destroy the energy. Special note, for curses it is recommended not to use your fireplace or a fire on your property.

Glass-Encased Candles

When I was in the Cayman Islands, some of the Voodoo practitioners reused the glass candle by throwing boiling water into the glass to remove any residual wax, and then cleansed it with Florida water. They would then mold a new candle by melting normal paraffin shop candles. If you have to discard the glass, do so responsibly. Never bury it where people or wildlife are passing by, especially for banishing or curse spells. An abandoned property might be a place. A better option than burying it is to take the glass to a recycling place the same as you would do for leftover wax.

Apartments

If you live in an apartment, you can have a large potting plant near your front door and one at the back of the apartment. Treat them as you would the front or back yard of a house and bury positive leftover wax here. For positive glass-encased candle spells, use the leftover glass holder as a pot for plants that have the same properties as the spell.

Some practitioners make their own graveyard to bury curse leftover wax and items in. Take a lidded basket or box, and place a white cloth in it that is large enough so that the four corners of the cloth stick out of the container when the lid is closed. Next, get enough graveyard dirt from a cemetery itself to cover the bottom of the cloth. Remember to ask permission from the Angel of Death and those spirits that protect the cemetery, as well as to leave nine pennies or coins at the gate and some sweats as you leave the cemetery. Normally, only a few handfuls are needed. Now, place the wax and other items in the basket after a spell. Place liquids into another container so they do not wet the cloth. On St. John's day, June 24th, take the cloth and tie the four corners, then go to a place away from your home where you can burn the items inside the cloth. Note, do not keep this box in your home.

Final Note

Do remember to clean your altar of negativity by either washing it with Florida water, or spraying Florida water or another cleanser over it. At the very least, spray some saltwater over it. This is very important if you did a banishing, binding, hex-breaking, reversing, or other curse spells. You do not want that energy to affect your prosperity or love spell.

Chapter 8: Color

Our perception of color is the brain's interpretation of the vibration of light waves reflecting off the candle. A white object reflects all the visible wavelengths of light back at you, making the object appear white. A black object absorbs the wavelengths, reflecting nothing, making the object appear to be a hole in space. In between these two extremes, are objects that reflect different wavelengths of light, making them appear to have color. Each color has a unique vibrational frequency, thus the color of a candle can greatly aid in your spellcasting.

However. This is not essential as it only adds to the power of your spell. In a pinch, you can use white in place of any color, and imagine it is the color you need. You may even write the color's name on the white candle for added effect. When using color in a spell, you are using the element light, in your spell. The element fire is from the flame, and earth from any herbs and the candle wax. Burn incense to add the element air.

Each color represents a principal or area that it is used for. Following are the general guidelines for color candle use. When using color candles, always make sure the candles are one solid color throughout and not dipped or sprayed candles. If in doubt, scratch a small amount of wax off the candle or ask the shop. Note that some reversing candles are black outside with the red inside.

Black

Day: Saturday.
Ruled By: Saturn.
Banishing, leaving a relationship, acknowledging grief, forgiveness, hexing, cursing, jinxing, protection, repelling or absorbing negativity, binding, shape-shifting, confusion, uncrossing, hex breaking, curse breaking, reversing, destroying evil, healing very powerful illnesses, endings, releasing, fertility, dark moon spells, repelling dark magic and negative thought-forms.

Blue

Day: Thursday.
Ruled By: Jupiter.
Element: Water.
Direction: West.
Creates confidence, most powerful protection color, evil eye, discover the truth, expand mental horizons, success, good fortune, removes blockages in communication, wisdom, spiritual inspiration, creativity, healing, peace, happiness, psychic growth, honor, loyalty, tranquility, astral projection, losing weight, harmony, health, luck, and dreams.

Brown

Locating lost objects, justice spells, home protection, pet protection, money, ideas, balance, influence friendships, special favors, neutrality, uncertainty, hesitation, concentration, telepathy, protection of familiars, animal magic, earth magic, studying, wealth, success, psychic powers, endurance, attract money, and financial success.

Copper

Passion, money goals, professional growth, fertility in business, career moves, spells for children, and wealth.

Dark Blue

Element: Water.
Direction: West.
Depression, changeability, the subconscious, healing, slow change, vulnerability, the goddess, inspiration, truth, dreams, protection, fidelity, deep emotions, peace, and meditation.

Gold

Worldly achievement, wealth, recognition, long life, the god, promotes winning, happiness, humor, cosmic influences, solar deities, success, masculinity, joy, fast luck, confidence, healing, fortune, intuition, attracts higher influences, divination, and victory.

Gray

Compromises, invisibility, settling negative emotions, neutrality, stalemate, negativity, neutralizes negative energies, non-nature faerie magic, travel to other worlds, and competition.

Green

Day: Friday.
Ruled By: Venus.
Element: Earth.
Direction: North.
Healing, gardening, growth, good harvest, prosperity, money spells, luck, earth mother, physical healing, monetary success, abundance, fertility, tree and plant magic, personal goals, employment, youth, ambition, greed, jealousy, earth, and the goddess.

Greenish Yellow

To give or remove the following; jealousy, anger, discord, sickness, cowardice, and anger.

Indigo

Karma, restoration of balance, meditation, protection against magic cast against you, spirit communication, ancient wisdom, neutralize magic cast against you, ward slander and lies.

Lavender

Spiritual development, psychic growth, divination, protection, peace, and blessings.

Light Blue

Tranquility, patience, health, understanding, healing, happiness, psychic awareness, intuition, creating opportunities, depression, safe journey, harmony in the home, and peace.

Magenta

Quick change, spiritual healing, use it to speed up spells by burning it with other candles (has a very high vibrational frequency), and exorcism.

Orange

Fertility, creative growth, self-esteem, confidence, energy, business goals, success, justice, legal matters, action, attraction (pulling things to you), happiness, business deals, power, luck, healing, and sudden changes.

Pink

Love, romance, friendship, affection, quiet sleep, rekindling trust, attracting new friends or lovers, healing of emotions, peace, affection, caring, compassion, and honor.

Purple

Day: Wednesday.
Ruled By: Mercury.
Chakra: Third Eye.
Element: Soul or the Spirit.
Meditation, sex, passion, commanding, domination, higher consciousness, past-life work, divination, astral travel, psychic protection, clearing up karma, preventing nightmares, influencing people in high places, psychic ability, spiritual power, self-assurance, hidden knowledge, power, business progress, ambition, success, confidence, protection, contact with the spirit world, healing, break bad luck, and drive evil away.

Red

Day: Tuesday.
Ruled By: Mars.
Element: Fire.
Direction: South.
Chakra: Base or Root.
Courage, healing, anti-evil eye, increase life force, determination, fast action, sexual passion, potency, survival, physical health, strength, pleasure, willpower, energy, lust, blood of the moon, love, sex magic, willpower, protection, conquer fear or laziness, and the god.

Silver

Divination, awakening psychic abilities, astral projection, invoking the goddess, intuition, repressing unwanted psychic powers or visions, dreams, astral energies, communication, moon magic, remove negative forces, open astral gates, meditation, protection, money, success, balance, wards off negativity, removes negative energy, reflecting of negative energy, and victory.

Silver Grey

Cancellation, neutrality, and stalemate.

Violet

Self-improvement, intuition, success in searches, and creativity.

White

Day: Monday.
Ruled By: Moon.
Element: All.
Protection, creativity, lunar spells, cleansing, divination, healing, contacting the gods, clear vision, spirituality, the goddess, peace, higher self, purity, purification, truth, dawn, sincerity, meditation, and substitute for any color.

Yellow

Day: Sunday.
Ruled By: Sun.
Element: Air.
Direction: East.
Mental exercise, love, romance, power, prosperity, gaining approval, memory, concentration, sharpen logic, the sun, intelligence, breaking mental blocks, divination, travel, attraction, charm, action, inspiration, creativity, studying (accelerates learning), change, harmony, clairvoyance, protection, and confidence.

Astral Colors

Primary color in bold, secondary color in italics, optional color.
Aquarius (Jan 20 - Feb 18) **Blue /** *Green* / Any color.
Pisces (Feb 19 - Mar 20) **White** / *Green* / Mauve.
Aries (Mar 21 - April 19) **White** / *Pink* / Red.
Taurus (April 20 - May 20) **Red** / *Yellow* / Green.
Gemini (May 21 - June 21) **Red** / *Blue* / Yellow.
Cancer (June 22 - July 22) **Green** / *Brown* / Silver.
Leo (July 23 - Aug 22) **Red** / *Green* / Orange.
Virgo (Aug 23 - Sep 22) **Gold** / *Black* / Yellow.
Libra (Sep 23 - Oct 22) **Black** / *Blue* / Pink.
Scorpio (Oct 23 - Nov 21) **Brown** / *Black* / Red.
Sagittarius (Nov 22 - Dec 21) **Gold** / *Red* / Purple.
Capricorn (Dec 22 - Jan 19) **Red** / *Brown* Black.

Days of the Week Color

Sunday: Gold, yellow, orange, and white.
Monday: Silver, white and gray.
Tuesday: Red and orange.
Wednesday: Purple, orange, light blue, grey, yellow, and violet.
Thursday: Blue, purple, royal blue, and indigo.
Friday: Green, pink, and aqua.
Saturday: Black, grey, and indigo.

Chapter 9: Herbs, Incense and Oils

Herbs, incense, and oils when used with spells add additional power to your spells, and in cases can be used on their own to do spells without the need for burning a candle, such as incense sticks, oils and herbs burned on a charcoal block, or herbs and oils used with bath salts.

Take care when burning herbs on a charcoal block or using a smudging stick as many plants (if not all) smell quite different when being smoldered. Sweet scents, turn sour very fast and the smell can go into clothing and other material.

Herbs

You can achieve almost any magical intent by sprinkling enchanted herbs and powders around your home or business, or burning them. Herbs and herb powders are traditional American and African folk magic, as well as hoodoo and voodoo, and are powerful and effective for creating change. Scattering blends of herbs or wearing a mojo bag with herbs are common methods of magic. Combining this with a candle spell greatly enhances your powers.

Many practitioners use herbs mixed with coarse sea salt, Himalia pink salt, or Epson salt to cleanse themselves before casting a spell. To cleanse an area before casting a spell, herbs are burned on a charcoal block or a smudge stick is lit and left to smolder. You can even dust your altar with herb powder to enhance your magical work. Alternatively, blow a small amount of powdered herb into the air to spread their magical influence through a room or place.

Herbs can easily be added to a candle after a layer of oil has been added by simply rolling the candle in dried herbs after anointing the candle, or sprinkling herbs and powder onto the candle.

For easier use, ground the herbs into a powder using a mortar and pestle. As you grind the herb, envision what the herb is for. This way, you will add your own energy and vibration to that of the herb, making a more potent mix.

Following is a short list of herbs you can use for different needs; feel free to blend different herbs to make your own blend. There are many more herbs that can be substituted, ask your local magic shop for assistance in what they sell.

Alertness: Black Pepper, Juniper Berry, Lemon, Peppermint, Pine, Rosemary, Rose Geranium, and Ylang Ylang.
Banishing: Carnation, Rue, and Frankincense.
Business: Cinnamon and Patchouli.
Congestion: Eucalyptus, Lavender, Lemon, Patchouli, Peppermint, Pine, and Rosemary.
Depression: Chamomile, Clary Sage, Eucalyptus, Juniper Berry, Lavender, Petitgrain, Rosemary, and Sandalwood.
Divination: Bay Laurel, Thyme, Sandalwood, Nutmeg, Lemon Grass, Acacia, Lilac, Lotus, and Narcissus
Fertility: Oak, Pine, and Rose.
Healing: Apple, Cinnamon, Sage, and Lavender.
Love: Jasmine, Lavender, Rosemary, Rose, Apple Blossom, Gardenia, Jasmine, and Ylang-Ylang.
Luck: Basil, Bayberry, and Vervain.
Memory: Cedarwood, Marjoram, Peppermint, and Rosemary.
Mental Powers: Caraway, Clove, Rue, and Honeysuckle.
Money: Almond, Basil, Cloves, Mint, Sage, Cinnamon, and Patchouli.
Pain-Relieving: Cajeput, Chamomile, Ginger, Helichrysum, Lavender, Marjoram, Rosemary, Clove, and Rose.
Peace: Basil, Frankincense, Rose, and Valerian.
Prosperity: Mint, Basil, Vervain, Hyssop, Bergamot, Cinnamon, and Patchouli.
Protection: Bay Laurel, Dill, Fennel, Fern, Rue, White Sage, Frankincense, Rosemary, Dragon's Blood, Bergamot, Cinnamon, Cinquefoil, and Sandalwood.
Purification: Anise, Pine, Rosemary, Bay Laurel, Frankincense, Benzoin, Sandalwood, Myrrh, and Rose.
Relaxation: Chamomile, Clary Sage, Juniper Berry, Lavender, Lemon, Mandarin, Marjoram, Neroli, Rose, Rose Geranium, Sandalwood, and Ylang Ylang.

Sex: Cinnamon, Patchouli, Lavender, Clove, Musk, Vanilla, and Tuberose
Skin-Rejuvenation: Carrot Seed, Frankincense, Lavender, Jasmine, Myrrh, Neroli, Palmarosa, Patchouli, and Rose.
Youth: Oak, and Sage.

Following is a list of herbs that are associated with each day of the week. When doing spells, you can add these herbs to your candle or burn them separately as incense or on a charcoal block.

Monday: Night Flowers, Willow Root, Orris Root, Birch, Motherwort, Vervain, White Rose, and White Iris.
Tuesday: Red Rose, Pine, Daisy, Thyme, and Pepper.
Wednesday: Fern, Lavender, Hazel, Cherry, and Periwinkle.
Thursday: Cinnamon, Beech, Buttercup, Coltsfoot, and Oak.
Friday: Pink Rose, Ivy, Birch, Heather, Clematis, Sage, Violet, and Water Lily.
Saturday: Myrrh, Moss, Hemlock, Wolfsbane, Coltsfoot, Nightshade, and Fir.
Sunday: Marigold, Heliotrope, Sunflower, Buttercup, Cedar, Beech, and Oak.

Essential Oils

Essential oils are extracted from flowers, fruits, bark, roots, and leaves of aromatic plants and are a concentrated form of the plant's energy. Using essential oil adds considerable power to your spell by utilizing the stored energy of the plant. Know that pure essential oil is normally irritating to the skin, and should be diluted with a carrier oil such as almond or grapeseed oil, or another carrier oil. When you apply oil to your body, it penetrates the skin and travels through the body where it affects the body according to the properties of the oil. When you burn oil in an oil diffuser or on a candle, it affects your mood according to the properties of the oil and can help focus your subconscious towards your goal.

Allspice, birch, camphor, cinnamon, clove, oregano, savory, thuja, thyme, turmeric, and wintergreen in pure essential oil are potentially toxic so be careful when working with them.

Know that many aromatherapy oils are not pure oil but synthetic, which may smell nice but have no magical energy. Even those that are made from real plants are already diluted. Make sure the container says essential oil.

When buying essential oil, buy from a reputable dealer as some essential oils are already diluted. Make sure the container is dark to keep out sunlight and that the oil was stored in a cool dark place.

Do know that essential oils have a shelf life, and are best used within a few years of manufacture. Look for expire and manufacture dates on the container before you buy it. However, in saying that, some oils do get more potent over the years up to a point, just like wine. These include but are not limited to, jasmine, rose, patchouli, and sandalwood.

For basic use, the list of usages for herbs is the same for essential oil as the oil is just a more concentrated form of the herb.

Following is a compressed list of essential oils that are associated with each day of the week.

Monday: Jasmine, Lemon, and Sandalwood.
Tuesday: Basil, Coriander, and Ginger.
Wednesday: Benzoin, Clary Sage, Eucalyptus, and Lavender.
Thursday: Clove, Lemon Balm, Oakmoss, and Star Anise.
Friday: Cardamom, Palmarosa, Rose, and Yarrow.
Saturday: Cypress, Mimosa, Myrrh, and Patchouli.
Sunday: Cedar, Frankincense, Neroli, and Rosemary.

Incense Sticks

Incense sticks are often used to purify a space before magical workings. White sage, lavender, rosemary, and frankincense are good choices for this purpose. However. Incense sticks come in a variety of purpose-blended packages, which can aid your spell work. You can for instance, burn a success incense to add to the chance of your spell working, or an attract money incense with a prosperity spell.

At its most basic, incense sticks are powdered herbs that are mixed with a resin gum to keep it together, and then rolled around a wooden stick. When burned, the stored energies of the herbs are released, mix with your energy and intent, and enter the metaphysical world to alter the physical world according to your intent. It is a more convenient but potentially less powerful way of burning herbs on a charcoal block. Interestingly, just like with essential oils, the smell from the incense sticks alters your mood, and you can, in fact, do a spell with only incense sticks.

Following is a list of popular incense that corresponds to each day of the week.

Monday: African Violet, Honeysuckle, Myrtle, Willow, and Wormwood.
Tuesdays: Dragon's Blood, and Patchouli.
Wednesday: Jasmine, Lavender, and Sweet Pea.
Thursday: Cinnamon, Musk, Nutmeg, and Sage.
Friday: Strawberry, Sandalwood, Rose, Saffron, and Vanilla.
Saturday: Black Poppy Seed and Myrrh.
Sunday: Lemon, and Frankincense.

Chapter 10: When to Start Your Candle

Although spells can be done at any time they are needed, there are optimal days and times during the months that can enhance your spell. For example, love spells are more powerful on a Friday in June.

Monthly Correspondences

Each month, just as each day, has its own theme and certain spells fare better when done during these months. However. Do not let that stop you from casting a spell. If you need to pay the bills, do your spell regardless of the month or day.

January

Name: Wolf Moon.
Safety, protection, cleansing, new beginnings, letting go of the past, and letting go of old karma.

February

Name: Ice Moon.
Forgiveness, healing, motivations, soul searching, and spiritual growth.

March

Name: Worm Moon.
Success, banishment of blockages, prosperity, new beginnings, expanding, and travel.

April

Name: Growing Moon.
Good luck, openings, banishment of blockages, prosperity, growth, starting projects, and opportunity.

May

Name: Hare Moon.
Development, growth in all aspects, and love.

June

Name: Mead Moon.
Commitment, understanding, balance, and love.

July

Name: Hay Moon.
Authority, self-regulation, planning the future, and self-assessment.

August

Name: Corn Moon.
Accord, peace, symmetry, letting go of hurt and old karma or habits, forgiveness, and starting anew.

September

Name: Harvest Moon.
Spiritual development and growth, completion of projects, tying up loose ends, cleaning your slate, reaping rewards, and planning for the future.

October

Name: Blood Moon.
Personal modifications, begin new projects, creativeness, a fresh start, letting go of old karma and grudges or habits.

November

Name: Snow Moon.
Empathy, personal assessment, re-evaluating your life, self-honesty, and planning for the future.

December

Name: Cold Moon.
Discernment, understanding of universal truths, letting go of unnecessary karma and habits, finding new ideas and ways to do things, out with the old and in with the new, and starting new innovative projects.

Day of the Week Correspondences

If possible, try to do your spells on the day during the week that corresponds to what your wish is. Just like months, each day during the week has a different energy that can enhance your spell. Following are the general correspondences for each day of the week.

Monday

Planet: Moon.
Metal Associated to Planet: Silver.
Star Sign: Cancer.
Angel: Gabriel.
Color: White.
Key Words: Psychic abilities, emotions, feminine matters, intuition, healing, protection, memory, purity, gaining confidence, clairvoyance, voyages, dreams, astral travel, merchandise, divination, inspiration, psychic awakening, new ideas, and starting projects.

Tuesday

Planet: Mars.
Metal Associated to Planet: Iron.
Star Sign: Aries and Scorpio.
Angel: Samuel.
Color: Red.
Key Words: War, courage, sexual matters, action, loyalty, wealth, power, passion, boost confidence, revenge, surgery, breaking negative spells, prison, lust, hunting, competition, politics, dark magic, and creating discord.

Wednesday

Planet: Mercury and Chiron (a moon of Pluto).
Metal Associated to Planet: Mercury or Zink.
Star Sign: Virgo.
Angel: Raphael.
Color: Purple.
Key Words: Communication, inspiration, creativity, mental abilities, business, travel, humor, self-expression, granting information, divination, writing, study, knowledge, business transactions, debt, luck, fear, job and career spells, self-improvement, and money spells.

Thursday

Planet: Jupiter.
Metal Associated to Planet: Tin.
Star Sign: Sagittarius and Pisces.
Angel: Sachiel.
Color: Blue.

Key Words: Abundance, money matters, politics, ambition, success, protection, honor, generosity, very good for prosperity, luck and success spells (waxing moon), happiness, riches, leadership, and legal matters.

Friday

Planet: Venus.
Metal Associated to Planet: Copper.
Star Sign: Libra and Taurus.
Angel: Ariel.
Color: Green.
Key Words: Love, sex magic, fertility, friendship, compassion, union, new projects, romance, marriage, pleasure, comfort, luxury, arts, music, and matters of the heart.

Saturday

Planet: Saturn.
Metal Associated to Planet: Lead.
Star Sign: Capricorn and Aquarius.
Angel: Cassiel.
Color: Black.
Key Words: Spirit Communications, meditation, psychic attack or defense, locating lost objects, protection, knowledge, legal matters, court spells, obstacles, delays, patience, hard work, real estate, banishing, bindings, reincarnation, karmic lessons, wisdom, starting long-term projects, prosperity, endings such as bad habits or karma or enemies.

Sunday

Planet: Sun.
Metal Associated to Planet: Gold.
Star Sign: Leo.
Angel: Michael.
Color: Yellow.
Key Words: Truth, growth, uplifting the spirit, advancements, enlightenment, rational thought, exorcism, healing, prosperity, hope, money, leadership, protection, creativity, success, travel, truth, friendships (no love spells), depression, job spells, peace, healing, and divine guidance.

Moon Cycle

If you work with the moon, then it is best to observe the cycle of the moon. However. Even if you do not work with moon energy, it can still help to follow the cycle of the moon for added effect.

New Moon

The new moon is when the moon is not visible. Spells can be done from new moon up until three and a half days after it starts.
Key Words: Quests, personal growth and cleansing rituals, new beginnings or ventures, purification, blessings, health, love, romance, and job searching.

Waxing Moon

The waxing moon occurs three and a half days after the new moon. Spells can be done up to ten and a half days from the new moon. However. To get the maximum effect, spells should be done just after new moon at the start of the waxing moon.
Key Words: Growth in anything from friendships to finances, fertility, communication, legal matters, healing, love, success, wealth, courage, luck, protection, wisdom, divination, strength, any spell where you want to increase or obtain something.

Full Moon

On full moon, the moon's power is at its strongest and is the best time for any positive spell, especially protection spells. The second day of full moon is especially good for finances. The sixth day of full moon is seen as a very good day for travel and travel spells. The seventh day is seen as a very lucky day, especially towards love. Human emotions are at their peak during full moon, and can cause people to fall in love easier.
Key Words: Enlightenment, ideas, commitments, protection (best time), divination, love, legal undertakings, knowledge, prophetic dreams, money, healing, blessing, health, fertility, wisdom, intuition, and friendship.

Waning Moon

The waning moon occurs three and a half days after full moon. Spells can be done up to ten and a half days from the full moon. However. To get the maximum effect, spells should be done just after full moon at the start of the waning moon.
Key Words: Repelling, clear out, banishing, bindings, endings, letting go, breaking spells, break ups, hex and curse breaking.

Blood Moon

There is a lot of confusion surrounding blood moons. A blood moon occurs during full moon when there is a lunar eclipse. During full moon when an eclipse occurs, the sun's light passes through the earth's atmosphere. The light is filtered and refracted due to dust and other particles in the atmosphere. Much of the green to violet light is removed, leaving more red light to hit the moon, making it appear red. See lunar eclipse for spells to cast.

Blue Moon

A blue moon is traditionally the second full moon in the same month. Spells related to a normal full moon can be done. Some see this moon as extra powerful, but in fact, it is the same as a normal full moon. Two full moons occur in the same month because the lunar cycle of just over 28 days is less than the days in a month. Occasionally a full moon will occur just at the start as well as at the end of a month.

Super Moon

Super moons are exceptionally powerful times. A super moon is a full moon, where the earth and the moon are closer together than normal. The moon may be from 7% to 30% brighter in the sky, and using this time gives you added energy. Apart from having more moon energy, it is the same as a normal full moon.

Dark Moon

The dark moon is for going to war. This time is exceptionally powerful in dealing with enemies and breaking curses. The dark moon phase is around two to three days before new moon and is similar in appearance (no moon).

Key Words: War, destruction of enemies, breaking of curses, bindings, banishing, hex and curse breaking, cursing spells, justice, and hexing spells.

Lunar Eclipse

A lunar eclipse happens when the earth moves between the sun and the moon. The earth's shadow then falls onto the moon, and blackens it out totally on a full eclipse and partially on a partial eclipse. A lunar eclipse happens during full moon at night, and can last for several hours for a full eclipse. The night would be dark (at the time of a full eclipse), while there is a full moon.

As the moon is actually full and at its strongest, you are working with full moon energy. However. If you use the time when the moon is eclipsed in your area, especially a full eclipse, the full moon energy combines with the dark moon. This is an exceptionally good time for war and breaking spells and curses, or letting go of things.

Solar Eclipse

A solar eclipse occurs during the day, on a new moon. It is seen as a super new moon for casting spells. The moon moves in between the sun and the earth, and blocks out part of the sun's light. A solar eclipse does not last very long, often only minutes, as well as that it is often only visible in a few places around the world. However. You do not need to see the eclipse to work with the energy, just observe when it occurs for your location. As you are working during the new moon, you are working with new moon energy. However. As it is daytime, you are working with the sun's energy as well. For this reason, this time is often seen as a very good time to start new projects, break bonds, and remove obstacles. Some use the time when there is no sun to do exceptionally strong dark magic. If you do magic at the eclipse, know that it does not last long, so burning herbs on charcoal or taking a quick herb bath are suggested over trying to burn a candle. If you do want to burn a candle at this time, burn a birthday cake candle that burns down quickly.

Harvest Moon

The harvest moon is the full moon closest to the autumnal equinox, either before or after 23 September. Normally, it occurs in September, but it can occur in October. Normal full moon spells can be cast. However. Any spells where you are to reap the rewards of your efforts have extra power during this time. Use the Jera and Fehu runes together for added effect.

Chapter 11: Interpreting Candle Flames

The magnetism of a candle flame is spell bounding, for it is a secret magical language. From the chapter, The Science Behind The Light, we have seen how a candle flame behaves in different ways. Now, we will look at what messages the candle may be giving.

Lychnomancy is a branch of Pyromancy, and a form of divination by candle flame. Often three candles are used. However. One candle can also be used. The same principle is used when looking at the flame for a spell candle. Although there are many technical reasons why a flame would behave in a certain way, it does not explain why candles of the same batch and burned together, behave differently.

Even if there is a technical reason for your candle to behave a certain way, it may have been preordained that you used that candle. The moment you decide to do a spell, the spell has already begun, and the results of the spell are already forming in the universe. For magic is in essence, thought, and you have already made your choice. The candle you select, whether flawed or perfect, may be the universe's way of answering your request.

When reading candle flames, the first thing one has to ensure is that there is no draft through the room and that the candle is of good quality. If only one candle is used in a spell, a white control candle may be burned alongside the spell candle to assert any outside influences. Although the candle flame may burn a certain way due to mechanic faults in the candle, many times, the changing state of the flame is due to influences on a different plane.

As the candle acts as a messenger to the spirit realm, forces there may affect the running of the spell. Almost like working with the aura of the candle. These effects will then be duplicated in the real world. In fact, only small changes in the flow of candle wax are needed to affect the candle flame drastically.

Slightly cooling the top of the candle will result in the wax melting slower; resulting in the flame burning lower, until it possibly dies. Heating the top of the candle slightly will result in the wax melting faster, creating more fuel for the flame. This will result in the flame burning higher until it starts to smoke and by itself melt the candle away. Even magnetic forces and vibrations can affect the candle flame, all, possible for spiritual beings.

Just like dream interpretation, nothing is absolute across the board, and one should take the results in light of the spell done and the current situation of the practitioner. Over time, you will learn how the particular candle brand you are using burns naturally. You will also learn how your guides send messages through the candle flame to you, and how to read your personal spell results. However. Following is a list of generally agreed-on messages for the behavior of a candle flame. For each, the magical interpretation and the possible scientific explanation are given. This will help you understand if it is a message (like a bad sign from a candle exploding), or from a faulty candle, or your fault (putting the candle in the freezer before use).

A Clean, Steady, and Strong Burn

Magical Interpretation:

A steady flame that burns strong is seen as a very good sign. Your spell has a very high chance of success, and the results should last a long time. If your spell is a petition spell where you asked a deity to do the work for you, then the deity has heard and is accepting to do the work (note that their acceptance has no relation to if they will be successful in their task).

Scientific Interpretation:

The candle is of good quality and there is no draft near the candle.

A Slow, Weak Burn

Magical Interpretation:

Your energy may not be focused correctly; your request is too vague or too long, or you may not have placed enough energy into the spell. There may be opposition (watch if the flame jumps) to your request, either from the universe, a person working against you, or the deity you petitioned is not agreeing to your request.

Channel more energy into your candle by focusing on the flame and concentrate on exactly what you want. If the flame grows larger, things are looking up for your spell. Continue putting energy in until it burns steady and strong. If you wrote on the candle or placed a paper under it, you may not be able to change the spell mid-burning and will need to reword the next spell better.

Scientific Interpretation:
The wick may be too thin for the size of the candle. The wax may be too hard or of poor quality. You started the candle with a too-short wick, causing it not to be able to get enough heat going to melt the wax properly. If the candle is in a holder, then there may not be enough air getting to the flame (typical of thin and tall glass candles). There may be too much or the wrong kind of color or fragrance added to the candle, as well as oil or herbs on the candle that is clogging the wick and stopping the flow of wax. Debris at the base of the wick can also clog the wick.

Hissing, Sizzling, Crackling, or Popping

Magical Interpretation:
Spirits may be trying to communicate or work with you, or the person you are directing the spell towards is answering you back. If you are doing a spell against another (cursing, binding, reversing spell, and so on) the person may be actively fighting back and cursing you back. If it is a healing spell, the person may be thanking you, or the spirit guides may be telling you that their sickness is their karma. Look at the flame for more information, as well as close your eyes and try to listen to your inner voice for more information.

Scientific Interpretation:
The wax is of poor quality or was not mixed properly. Herbs and oil placed into, on, or around the candle may be catching fire. The wick is of poor quality. Too much coloring or fragrance was used in the candle making (especially homemade candles). The candle may have gotten wet and moisture went into the wick (can happen, if a candle is left in a fridge or frozen).

An Unsteady, Jumping, Sputtering, or Flickering Flame

Magical Interpretation:

There is resistance against your spell. The higher the flame jumps, the larger the resistance against your spell. This may indicate a curse on you (especially if you try to do a protection or prosperity spell). If you are doing a spell against another, including a reversing spell, they may be actively fighting back. In all cases, put more energy into your spell while focusing on your intent.

Scientific Interpretation:

There may be a draft around the candle. Flickering occurs when the teardrop shape of the flame is disturbed. Even walking slowly by a candle can cause the flame to flicker. See if it settles in a minute or so after standing dead still. The wick may be of bad quality and not allowing the wax to flow consistently to the top of the wick. The wax may be of bad quality and not melting consistently, or too much coloring or sent was added to the candle. Herbs placed in, on, or around the candle may be catching fire. The candle may have gotten wet and moisture went into the wick (can happen, if a candle is left in a fridge or frozen).

Puffs of White Smoke

Magical Interpretation:

Your request is granted. White smoke is normally a good sign that your intentions are heard and may be granted. However. Realize that the message is given for circumstances at the moment, and if an adversary hears you are progressing forward, they may counter your spell. So keep your good news to people you trust.

Scientific Interpretation:

The white smoke you see from a candle, often after the flame goes out, is not actually smoke. It is vaporized wax. Often you can smell the wax. The wax is only flammable when it is vaporized. As the candle melts, the wax is vaporized and travels up the wick where it ignites. If the flame dies or the temperature drops too much, the vaporized wax does not burn but some do still travel up the wick for a time after the flame dies, which looks like white smoke.

Puffs of Black Smoke

Magical Interpretation:
Black smoke is normally seen as a bad sign. There are forces at work against your spell. Black smoke normally comes with a large flame. The larger the flame, the more energy from the spell is consumed, and the larger the resistance is.

Scientific Interpretation:
The wax may be too soft, the room too hot, another candle is too close (min 3 inches apart), or the wick is too long. Any of these can result in the wax melting away too fast and creating a large flame. Leftover carbon molecules then leave the flame in the form of black soot, before they are properly burned. Additionally, the wax may be of poor quality, or too much color or sent was added to the candle. Herbs or oils added to, or placed onto the candle are catching fire. There may be a draft near the candle. If too little air reaches the candle flame, it will disturb the flame's teardrop shape, causing it to soot. This is especially true of large glass candles or when placing several candles close together, especially in a small space.

Vanishing Flame

Magical Interpretation:
Someone very powerful is working against you and has stopped your spell. The universe or your deity has rejected your request. Your wording is unclear or you have not charged the candle with enough energy. Try relighting the candle while adding more energy to the candle. If the candle dies again, and it is not a science problem listed below, let it go for a few days and then retry the spell or maybe a different spell with different wordings. If the candle burned almost all the way down and left ½ inch or more of wax, the spell needs to be repeated. If the flame is smothered by the wax, it is normally seen that your spell failed and your wish will not be granted.

Scientific Interpretation:
If the flame dies, a draft may have blown the flame out, especially if it was small, to begin with. Herbs, powder, candlewick burnt parts, or a foreign object may have clogged the wick and starved the flame of fuel (remove any if found and relight the candle). The wick may be of bad quality, or the wax may have impurities or color pigments that clogged the wick.

Self-Relighting Flame

Magical Interpretation:
Your intentions are still being considered by your spirits. There is still work to be done. Keep focusing. Your spell has broken through obstacles.

Scientific Interpretation:
When a candle flame dies, vaporized wax still travels up the wick and is sometimes seen as white smoke. Additionally, glowing embers can sometimes be seen in the wick. If the wick can heat the vaporized wax enough to cause combustion, the candle can relight itself. It sometimes happens when wind or a draft suddenly blows out the flame.

The Candle Doesn't Burn At All

Magical Interpretation:
There is too much resistance against you. The person you are doing a spell against has too powerful protection (happens with either cursing or reversing spells). Your spell is too weak to break the curse or hex. There is too much negativity in the room, clear it first. Your spell has been rejected by the universe or your deity you petitioned, or your heart is not in the spell. Refocus your energy, and try relighting the candle by holding the flame longer and meting some wax to help the candle on.

Scientific Interpretation:
The wick is too small for the candle size. Incorrect coloring or scent has been added to the candle that causes the wick to clog up and extinguish the flame. There is a foreign object (often a bug) at the base of the wick, blocking the flow of wax. The wick is too short and cannot melt enough wax to keep a flame.

Burning Only On One Side

Magical Interpretation:
Only half of your request may be granted. Try to refocus your energy or restate your request more clearly. Things may be left unresolved or unsettled, or you may need to add more power or do something yourself to have the total request granted. You may be attacking the problem from the wrong angle. Such as doing a hex-breaking candle when the evil eye is sent to you due to jealousy.

Scientific Interpretation:
The wick may be off-center in the candle. If so, find a better candle and try the process again for better results. A draft may be present within the room blowing the flame to one side causing it to melt away. Part of the wick or a foreign object such as a moth may have fallen into the wax and caught fire, causing a second flame. Another candle may be too close to the candle, causing the second candle's flame to melt one side of the candle away. The candle may be standing skew in the holder, a problem with thick candles.

Burning With Multiple Flames

Magical Interpretation:
Someone may be working either with or against you. You will need to examine the flames. If the flames are dancing together, it is normally seen as someone working with you. If they dance against each other (one goes up while the other goes down), it is normally seen as someone working against you. In either case, if there is black smoke, it is normally not a good sign, and if the original flame dies and the second one continues, it is normally a very bad sign. Traditionally, if it is a protection spell then the extra flames are enemies working against your spell. With controlling spells, it means your target has help working for them and against you or their protection is too strong. If it is a breakup or separation spell, it is an indication that the spell worked. However. If it is a love spell, it means the relationship would possibly break up, especially if there are three flames on a divination candle for a couple. The third flame represents the person trying to break up the couple. Two flames that work together on a love spell however is normally seen as a success.

Scientific Interpretation:
Part of the wick or a foreign object such as a moth may have fallen into the wax and caught fire, causing a second flame. On a too-long wick, high concentrations of carbon can form a ball in the wick. When a large mass of curled wick drops, it may form a second wick.

The Candle Cracks, Explodes, Sets Something Alight

Magical Interpretation:
Use extreme caution. A powerful spell caster or entity may be working against you. You may be under attack especially if the spell is a protection candle. Or if you are trying to affect another especially with a curse, their protection may be more powerful than your spell, and your spell bounced back at you. Do a clearing of yourself and your house. If the candle that broke was white, the candle may have taken the negativity for you. If something was set on fire, you may have more losses coming your way. Do a protection spell or take a bath in protection herbs and salts. If the candle or glass only cracks then there was some opposition or negativity was sent to you, but the candle absorbed it and broke through the resistance or the protection of the person you directed the spell towards. However. For reversing, hex-breaking, or uncrossing spells, if the candle, glass, or mirror cracks, then it is seen that the spell that was placed upon you, has been broken.

Scientific Interpretation:
The candle may have been of poor quality, especially a glass candle. Another candle may have been too close to the candle, especially a glass candle. You left things too close to the candle, and a draft caused it to catch fire. The candle was too cold. This can happen if you are doing it in a very cold room or outside in the cold or placed the candle in the fridge. Glass and large candles are especially vulnerable to cold. The glass holder was scratched or had a flaw in it.

The Candle Burns Away Very Fast

Magical Interpretation:
This usually goes with either a twin flame or a very large flame. If not, then it is often a fault in the candle making. A candle that burns away very fast indicates that results will be seen quickly, but often will not last.

For instance, a better business spell may see you with only an hour or a day of improved business, and then things may change back to normal. For a love spell, the guy or girl may call you once, and then ignore you afterward. If the wax just melted away, there may be a message in the wax for you.

Scientific Interpretation:
The candle wax is too soft or the room is too hot, resulting in the candle melting too fast, often resulting in a pile of leftover wax. The wick may be too large for the candle thickness, resulting in too much wax being burned at one time, resulting in a short candle life. In this case, the candle would actually be burning correctly taking the size of the wick. Thus, you have a fast-acting candle. It is good, as long as there are not piles of leftover wax. Candles placed too closely together can create their own draft. This can cause the candles to flare and melt away very fast. A too-long wick will cause a large flame and pull a lot of wax up, causing the candle to burn away very fast.

The Wick Makes a Knot

Magical Interpretation:
There are obstructions to your spell, and the spell is trying to burn through them. See if the knot is burned away and if another one forms. Someone may be placing obstacles in your path. If you use deities, you may petition them to help you remove the obstacles.

Scientific Interpretation:
The wick is of poor quality. The wick is too thick or long for the candle size. This allows too much wax to be pulled up the wick and carbon is building up on the wick creating a mushroom or knot. Be careful as the knot can separate from the wick, land on the top of the candle, and catch fire, causing a second flame. This will result in the candle melting away very fast. Immediately, but carefully, remove the extra flame with a fireproof item if it happens.

The Top of the Candle or Whole Candle Ignites

Magical Interpretation:
You may have used too much power for the candle, especially if you are doing a love or job spell. If doing a curse or hex, the spell may have backfired badly on you, and you have been set on fire. Someone very powerful is working against you. See if it settles down, if not, stop the candle and relight the wick.

Scientific Interpretation:
The wick is too large for the candle. The wax is too soft. You used too many herbs or oils with a low flashpoint (citrus fragrances are a problem), and the oil caught fire. Try a different oil, and use less of it as well as herbs and other oils. If you made your candle yourself, try a slightly smaller wick and add less fragrance to the candle. Using certain coloring may also cause problems. Color crayons are not a good way to make candles.

Reading the Smoke

Although the meanings for white and black smoke have been listed before, there are additional signs to look for.

1: When a non-encased candle smokes in the beginning but then clears up later, it means that there is hidden trouble. An enemy may be secretly working against you and that things may not go well in the beginning. However. If you persevere and keep working physically and with spell work towards your goals, you will overcome the obstacles or person.
2: If the candle smokes black when lit, then there is negativity around you and the candle is working to remove it. See how the candle performs later.
3: If the candle smokes white when lit, then your request is being answered, but you may have a struggle at first to get it.
4: If the smoke moves towards you, then your wish has a high chance of being granted and your wish is within reach. However. With black smoke, you may need to do some extra work. Keep pushing you are almost there.
5: If the smoke moves away from you, your goals are far, and you will need a great deal of work and perseverance to get what you want.

6: If the smoke moves to your right, then you are too emotional to pursue your wish. Stand back; look at your situation with a broad overview, and use logic and your head to gain success. It may take some patience to get where you want to be.
7: If the smoke moves to your left, then you are self-sabotaging yourself by being too emotionally involved in the situation. As with the smoke going right, use logic and a clear mind to look at your situation, else your wishes will not be answered.

Glass-Encased Candles

With glass-encased candles, there are a few added signs to look for.

The Glass Is Completely Black

If the spell is done and the glass is blackened by soot from top to bottom, then it is normally a sign that an evil spell or negativity was sent your way and may be stopping your spell, or that obstacles are blocking your spell.

For any spell apart from uncrossing, reversing, and hex-breaking, do an uncrossing spell and then redo the spell you originally did that burned black. The exception is for controlling spells (even love spells), as black soot is seen as a message that the spell may backfire on you, so stop your requests. If it was for a war spell such as uncrossing, revenge, reversing or curse and hex-breaker, then redo the spell to break through the opposition's defenses.

The Glass Is Black at the Top Only

Negative forces or another spellcaster was working against you. The darker the black and the deeper it goes down the candle, the stronger the opposition was and the longer they persisted. If the black stops before halfway down the candle, then it is normally seen as you won, any further down and some obstacles or negativity may remain. White soot from the middle down means the cleaning or curse breaker was successful.

The Glass Is Black at the Bottom Only

If only the bottom half is black, then it is normally seen that someone picked up on your spell and is sending negativity your way or working against you. The darker the black the stronger the resistance. This is especially true for any controlling or reversing spell. Depending on your spell, you may have difficulty ahead in obtaining your desires, especially for prosperity spells. Consider doing an uncrossing and protection spell. If there is white soot at the top half and black at the bottom, then evil or another person overrode your spell.

White Soot on the Glass All the Way

If the white soot goes all the way from the top to the bottom of the glass, then you may need more cleansing and may need to redo the spell if it was for banishing, hex breaking, or reversing. If for prosperity or job-related spells, then you may need more work on your part to obtain what you want.

If the soot goes all the way down, but is only on one side of the glass, then your spell was either incorrect or your current aim is not appropriate for you, and your guides are not happy.

Burn Marks on the Glass

If the flame burned the glass, especially if it melted or burned any labels on the outside of the glass, then enemies are stabbing you in the back. These can be people close to you sending hate and jealousy or even working actively against you. Do protection spells and wear protection against the evil eye.

Signs on the Glass

You may find images in either the black or the white residue left on the glass. This is much the same as reading leftover wax. Imagines that are threatening, such as skulls in the black soot, are seen as bad. Good images such as doves in white soot are seen as good signs. Use your intuition but do not get carried away as the overall burning of the candle determines the outcome.

Chapter 12: Interpreting Candle Wax

Many practitioners worry when a candle melts and does not burn all the wax. Although it is a good sign if all the wax is used up and only a small part of the wick remains, this is not needed for a spell to work.

Often, there is a lot of information to be read in the leftover wax. From who is working against you, to how effective the spell was. At times, it may take a bit of searching to see any patterns or figures in the wax and decipher their meaning, while at other times, the meaning will be as clear as daylight. In a way, the images need to be read like one reads tea leaves or coffee grounds.

It is always a good idea to take a few digital pictures of the leftover wax with a camera or cell phone. Often, you will only see figures later, or when you show the pictures to someone else. The pictures are also a good reference to see how your guides or the deity you petitioned is answering you. Place the pictures in a word document or diary book, with notes on what the spell was for and what you think the results were. Then months later, see how your life changed and how accurate you were with interpreting the wax. Add this information as well to serve as a future reference.

Do know that some candles, especially ones in glass containers or holders, are designed not to burn all the way down. This is to help protect the glass from cracking or shattering. However. If there is more than ½ inch of wax left above the end of the wick or bottom of the glass if it has no stopper, then the spell needs to be redone. Any wax left on the insides of the glass means that there may be personal hindrances and that the spell may need to be repeated, or you need to do more work to get what you want.

There is no definite meaning to images or figures you see in the wax. However. There are some generally accepted possibilities. These associations are only for freestanding candles that melt away and form piles at the bottom or in a candleholder.

Two Different Types of Images

Transient images are images that appear and then melt away as the candle burns. These images give you clues as to the real-time happenings. If you leave the candle unattended, you will miss them. It is a good idea to take digital pictures of the candle at various stages of the burning process.

Persistent images are images that remain in the wax when the spell is done. These are the ones people often see and may indicate the results of the spell, as well as what forces are working for or against you. It may also show forces that remained and are currently, or will interfere with your wishes.

Tears Running Down the Candle

A transient image that often forms during spell work and normally disappears when the spell is done, is wax droplets running down the side of the candle, called tears. It is understood that someone will cry or be hurt emotionally before the spell succeeds.

Tears that create hanging waterfalls or frozen drops usually indicate that it may require a lot of effort from you to get what you want and that there may be a lot of emotional pain. It could be you or people around you. Tears are seen as sorrow. The sorrow is thought to last as long as the tears. If the tears melt away before the spell is done, then the sorrow will pass in due time. Tears that remain when the spell is done indicate that the affected person will be emotionally hurt for a long time. The amount of tears indicates the amount of hurt.

Reading Images

Reading the images in the wax should be taken against the spell done. If hearts and babies form in a love candle, it is a good sign. So to skulls and coffins forming in a reversing or hex-breaking candle. Thus, if the image relates to the spell, it is good. However. If the image is the opposite of the spell, such as a skull in a love spell, or a dove in a reversing spell, it normally means bad.

Serpent-like strings in any candle normally indicate that evil is being neutralized. If the serpent remains when the spell is done, then some evil may have remained, and more work is needed. The spell may need to be repeated, or use a stronger spell.

If you see the shape of an eye, then it is a warning that someone is watching you and may be sending negativity in the form of hate, jealousy, and possibly spells. If the eye remains when the spell is done, the issue is not resolved. Consider doing an uncrossing and protection spell.

Any claws, tails, stingers or so, is seen as malicious, gossip, and backstabbing. Twisted pillars of wax, bizarre shapes, and monsters are seen as turbulence in healing spells and opposition in war spells, or hardship in prosperity spells. If it remains when the spell is done, the evil has remained or the person is not stopped. Repeat the spell until the wax burns clean of those images.

The following I can testify to myself as to getting, and the results. An uncrossing candle I did is pictured below. However. I have received many of these candles with the same results. If you get a hooded figure; it means that either Santa Muerte, the Holy Death (especially among Hispanic folk), or another death spell or total ruin has been invoked against you. Uncrossing and protection spells are necessary. From the image, the hooded figure is next to the center of the candle. Three times within a week, I almost wrote my car off, twice from trucks skipping red robots and almost taking me out, and once from a school bus that did the same. I did reverse candles on all occasions and eventually found the culprit when that person (close to me) later admitted to a mutual friend that she had a near-death experience, which I later correlated to the times I did the reversing candles. Her life is now in total ruin, and she lost everything she had as her spells backfired.

Hooded figure left in the wax after an uncrossing candle.

Animal figures in normal candles are usually a good sign, and often mean a spirit or totem is working with you. However. In war candles (banishing, hex-breaking, and so on), it often indicates that an animal was sacrificed in a spell against you (blood spell). Uncrossing, hex-breaking, and protection spells are necessary. Often, tallow candles (animal fat) are used in uncrossing blood spells. However. For those who practice black arts or voodoo or hoodoo, see a reputable psychic to make sure what needs to be done.

Melting of Wax

How the wax melts is also important. If it melts evenly, almost like a flower unfolding with even ridges, it is often seen as roads and paths are being opened and that there are possibilities for success. If the candle is very lopsided, and the wax melts a lot more on one side, you may be dealing with situations that are out of balance.

In love spells where two candles are used and the wax merges or firmly connects at the base, it is seen as a good sign. The relationship would most probably happen. If one candle melts over the over, the person the candle represents is clingy and more eager to have a relationship. This could result in an unbalanced relationship where the clingy person dominates the relationship, possibly leading to its breakup in the distant future.

With love spells, if the base does not connect or the wax does not merge, turmoil, arguments, and so on may result, stopping or breaking the union. The opposite is true if it was a separation spell. Connecting wax means they will fight but reunite, maybe even stronger than before, and not connecting wax is a good sign in this case.

Any wax leftover in a glass-encased candle means unresolved issues, and that the spell may only partly succeed. The exact unresolved issues depend on the spell. For instance. In a love spell, the target person may make advancements but then backs off. In a prosperity spell, it could mean you need to resolve issues first, or that things may start to go better and then slow down.

Pins in the Wax

When using pins in candle spells, the way they drop or cling is very important.

Pins that do not drop, but cling, are normally seen as that the person the spell is done for, is clinging to the past, or something does not want to let go of the person. If the candle is for you, then you may not want to let go of past memories, and it is holding you back (prosperity and business success spells), or an entity or person is unwilling to let you or the situation go (uncrossing and hex-breaking spells). The same goes for a person you are doing the spell for. For breakup spells, the couple or one person may cling to the other and may not be willing to let go.

Divination may be needed to see if it is memories, a person, or a spirit that is unwilling to let go, especially if you are doing a spell for another person that is not war-related (hex-breaking and so on), such as a prosperity spell. A person may subconsciously be holding themselves back due to hidden beliefs. If the problem is memories, then a cleansing Black Walnut bath may be needed, as well as possibly past-life regression if it seems it is part of your karma. If the problem is a person or spirit, then a cleaning Van Van bath is needed, as well as a spell using Cut and Clear Dressing Oil or a separation spell to get rid of the person or entity. For bad cases, Cast Off Evil and or Hot Foot Oil, and or Be Gone formulas may be needed. A final note. After all is said and done. Do not stress about the outcome of a spell, even if the candle cracked, the flame went out, or set something alight. Doing so will just add more negativity to a spell, and may make matters worse. Calmly take appropriate action. For spells that went well, let them be and do their thing. Worrying if they are working may hold the energy back. For detailed explanations on images, see a good book on tealeaf reading.

Pictured above, a justice spell done on a pedophile and child abuser. See the bucket 'spilling the beans' and the bird at the 7 o'clock position. He sang like a bird eight months after being arrested and split on his brother.

Chapter 13: Candle Myths and Facts

1: ***Storing a candle in a freezer will make it burn longer.***
A cold candle will burn more slowly, but it only takes a few minutes for the heat from the flame to warm the candle to room temperature. Therefore, the temperature of the room determines candle burn speed not putting it in a freezer. A candle that was in a freezer may crack and even split open from the sudden temperature change. Glass candles can shatter. Moisture in the freezer can go into the wick and cause the flame to sputter or die.

2: ***Never blow out a candle.***
Blowing out a candle is seen as blowing the spell away, and pinching the wick dead is seen as pinching the spell dead. However. Some spells that you do against another practitioner require you to forcefully blow out the candle as if you are blowing the other person's power out. In this case, blowing the candle out is okay. The concern is that tiny droplets of wax or a piece of the still-burning wick can be blown onto the surrounding area and cause damage. If you use your hand behind the candle flame as a shield, hot wax, or part of the burning wick can be blown onto your hand, or worse, blown back into your eyes.

3: ***You need to cut the wick ¼ inch before lighting it.***
It is highly recommended to cut the wick as a too-long wick can cause the flame to grow too long and flare, as well as cause soot. The large flame may also melt the candle away very fast, without burning up the wax. However. Good-quality wicks are self-trimming and will settle down very soon.

4: ***You have to have a candle to do a candle spell.***
This myth does not mean to do magic, but to do candle magic. If you do not have a candle and wish to do a candle spell, you can use your imagination and light a virtual candle. This does take a bit of imagination, but does work. Imagine how you would anoint and charge and light the candle, then visualize how it burns down correctly. When you charge the candle, actually move your hands as if you have a candle, and place energy into your virtual candle. Using this method, you can, in fact, create a very powerful spell that works quickly.

5: ***Everything has to be perfect.***
It is more important to have the right intent than special ingredients. Magic is all about thought, focus, and belief. The candles, herbs, oils, and other props are there to help you focus your energy as well as add a bit of extra power. However. The rarest herbs and oils will not work if you believe the spell will fail because you put 10 drops of oil in the mix instead of 9. Be flexible, and realize that you do not need all the ingredients and that everything does not have to be perfect for a spell to work. Your belief is stronger than having the right color candle or the rarest herb or getting the day and hour right.
6: ***Light all candles with a lighter or another candle.***
Although the use of matches dates back to AD 577 in a town in Northern China, the art was lost until 1826 when John Walker of England invented the first friction matches (a note in the text Cho Keng Lu, written in 1366, mentions the use of sulfur matches during the conquest of Northern Qi). Many practitioners see the Sulfur in the match head as disrupting to any spell. Others see its banishing quality as beneficial to reverse, banishing, and hex breaking spells. Regardless of your feelings towards the Sulfur, what is less known and maybe more important to practitioners, is that the binding agent or glue in the match head is animal glue. Animal glue is made through prolonged boiling of animal skins, bones, tendons, and other tissues. Although fish, rabbits, and other animals are used, the preferred animal is horses. Put down horses (killed) are often referred to as been 'sent to the glue factory'. It is your personal preference, and as long as you are happy with what you light a candle with, it is correct.
7: ***Write your spell using a magical alphabet or sigils.***
Many practitioners believe in writing their spell either on the candle or on paper in a magical or secret alphabet such as theban, enochian, malachain, etc. This is seen as focusing your spell, as well as keeping it secret. Some go as far as creating their own alphabet as they see it as a dedication. Using a common language is believed to not focus your energy correctly on the words in the spell, as you know the language too well.
However. I disagree with this practice. First, unless you know the alphabet you use by heart, you will have to keep looking up the correct letter for each letter in your spell as you write it. This will break your concentration on the actual spell. Second, again unless you can read the alphabet fluently, you will not be able to recite the spell effortlessly. In addition, if you became so fluent in your personal alphabet that you can

read it effortlessly, your focus is the same as using your home langue. Then, you have the problem of the universe trying to decipher what you want. Yes, years back Latin was the preferred spell language, but that is so old school, that English is the most widely used language and understood by just about any deity you could petition. This goes for sigils as well. Unless you create a sigil for a specific spell that you do over and over, a once-off sigil is not as powerful and could potentially be useless compared to just writing out your wish in your normal language that your guides understand. Remember, a personal sigil has meaning only to the spell caster. Sigils that are universal, like that of angels, draw upon the belief and power of all that have worked with them.

8: ***Paraffin wax is toxic.***

No. Paraffin wax is non-toxic. Only food-grade paraffin is used in candles. Furthermore, common candle materials, including paraffin wax are biodegradable.

Chapter 14: Tips

1: If possible, keep a few candles of your favorite color to use in stock under or near your altar. The candles will be charged with your vibrations and energy as you do other spells. Keeping frequently used candles in stock will also prevent you from needing to do an urgent spell only to find out the local store is sold out. Remember, around full and new moon, and any important religious days, candles sell out fast. However. Always cleanse the candles from negativity before storing or using them.

2: When you dress candles for a specific purpose, never use them for another spell. Wiping the oil and herbs off will not clear the charging and the spell may backfire on you. Rather get another candle. Unless specified in the spell, always let a candle burn down completely. If you do not have the time to let the candle burn all the way, do the spell another time or get a smaller candle. Stopping and restarting a candle is worse than getting a smaller candle. Each time you stop the candle, you stop the spell, and energy flow to it.

3: Do not use leftover wax to mold candles. The energy of the previous spell is still associated with the wax. Discard it responsibly.

4: Any color can be substituted for another color. Say you needed green that represents money and have yellow. State that the yellow represents the sun and abundance. A white candle can be used as if it is another color, even black. Simply state the candle represents the color you want and imagine the white candle as if you are using that color. Yes, you can do evil with white candles. So much for believing someone is good because you see him or her only burning white candles.

5: If you are unsure of doing a spell, take a white or black candle and designate it as a void candle. When doing your spell, light the void candle first. State that if your spell will cause harm to another, be rejected, or it goes against the wishes of the soul of the other person, that the energy of your spell should go to the void candle and the spell must not be granted. The void candle then takes all harm, even if your spell backfires. The void candle can burn down within minutes, a sure sign that someone would have been seriously hurt by your spell. If the void candle cracks or explodes, your spell may have backfired and the void candle took the damage.

Remember, harm can be extreme emotional harm that can manifest in physical harm. Often, this happens with love and controlling spells. The target of a love spell has his or her free will removed and is being controlled. They are being forced to love someone they do not. This causes extreme emotional distress that will result in physical distress later and often violence, normally towards the lover who did the spell or had it done by another.

6: A Mirror placed under a candleholder amplifies the spell if so intended, or reflects a spell send to you. A parabolic mirror will focus the spell's energy into a penetrating beam that cuts through all obstacles. Think of a reflective lens in a flashlight. Foil can also be wrapped around a glass holder candle to the same effect, as well as placed under the candleholder to create a mirror effect if a mirror is not available. Tea light candles are pre-wrapped.

7: Foil wrapped around a candle helps to protect the spell from interference, as well as amplify the power, much the same as a mirror. However. Only do this on glass candles or large wax candles as the foil will reflect the heat and may cause the candle to melt away. Watch out that the foil does not catch fire. Tea light candles are naturally covered in reflective holders and safer to use. They are powerful, easy to transport and store, easy to explain away, burn long enough to work but short enough not to draw attention, and come in several colors. If you need more candle power, put a few next to each other and burn them together. I have done 100 tea lights in one spell all at once.

8: Store candles in a cool, dark, and dry place, with tapers or long candles lying down to prevent them from warping.

9: Candle wax drippings on most candleholders are easier to remove if hot water is run over them. Be careful not to burn yourself. Wax stuck in a candleholder is easier to remove if the holder is placed into a freezer for an hour or so. The wax shrinks and easily pops out of the candleholder.

Chapter 15: Tarot Cards and Candles

Just like writing your wish or spell on a piece of paper and placing it under or next to the candle holder, so can you do with tarot cards. Tarot cards each have a universal message or theme, which have been around a long time.

When using tarot cards, the picture on the card must represent what you are aiming for, or what you associate with that card. As there are multiple meanings for each card, you cannot just walk into a store, pick any pack, and use its cards in spells. You have to work with the cards a bit and connect with them. You can use the list provided of what each card's keywords and theme are, or you can look at each card individually and decide what the card stands for you. Once you have decided on a card that represents your wish, maybe the lover's card to attract love, or the justice card to win a court case, burn the appropriate candle with the tarot card under or next to the candle holder. Be careful that the candleholder does not damage the card by getting too hot. A holder that has the candle away from the base is suggested; or rather place the card next to the holder.

Normally, only the 22 major arcana cards are used in candle magic and are listed here.

The Fool

The fool can be used to make opponents blind to the truth, normally in court cases, to have opposition appear childish and foolish, or it can be used as a travel card to help you just to go on impulse if you are stuck in a rut.
Key Words: Blind to the truth, impulsive, childlike, pure, uncorrupted, and impulsive travel.

The Magician

The magician is a good card to use if you need to be creative and come up with ideas for a project, write exams, or need to think of solutions, including spells for a problem. It can also be used with a dream candle to help you find answers and knowledge in dreams, as well as with a red candle for action, normally if you procrastinate too much.

Key Words: Initiative, action, conscious awareness, manifestation, knowledge, and focus.

The High Priestess

The high priestess can be used as a healing card, but more to see people's true intentions and motivations. It can also be used to help you enhance your magical talents, possibly with the use of the magician.
Key Words: Hidden feelings, secrets, intuition, feminine power, healer, the unconscious, hidden motivations, mysterious influences, and talents.

The Empress

The empress can be used in place of the magician as a creativity card, but is more used to help with depression and with the high priestess with healing. If combined with the coin cards, it can be used for abundance, but may be used on its own for abundance with visualization.
Key Words: Development, sensual pleasure, abundance, compassion, creativity, lifting spirits, and action.

The Emperor

The emperor is a power card and figure of control, and can be used to get your way in an argument, get a promotion, or to have others see your reasoning. In essence, a controlling card. If you are guilty, you may try to use it on the judge, but be careful for if the spell backfires, your punishment will be worse. The Empress with compassion towards you may be a safer and better spell to do.
Key Words: Power, leadership, power of reason, authority, laws and values, control, and rules.

The Hierophant

The hierophant mostly represents traditional knowledge and values, as well as a person teaching it. The card is often used when professional spiritual help or guidance is needed. You may use it with a white candle asking that a person of the knowledge you need crosses your path to help you with your problems.
Key Words: Holding back, respect, teaching traditional rules, discipline, peer pressure, and knowledge.

The Lovers

The lovers' card is possibly one of the most-used cards in candle magic, as it is mostly used in love spells. The card can be used with a lover candle to attract a lover to you, cause desire for you in a known person, or make you more attractive and tempting in general. Know that almost all love spells eventually end in disaster, especially when the power of the spell has worn off.
Key Words: Love, choice, temptation, commitment, and completeness.

The Chariot

The chariot is mostly about winning, and getting to the top. It can be used against an adversary, in court cases, and to beat the opposition. It can also be used to give you the willpower to keep going for your dreams. However. As with everything, it can be used for the darker side and curses. Due to its nature of going for the top regardless of the cost, it can be used to cause others to take risks that if unsuccessful, will cause their downfall. However. Know that if they succeed, not only have your plans failed but also you helped them to the top.
Key Words: Willpower, diligence, honesty, perseverance, success, win at all costs, victory, adventure, and risk-taking.

Strength

The strength card can be used with healing to give others or yourself the strength to recover. It can also be used to have the strength to keep going, or added to any spell to add strength to the spell if so intended. It can also be used that others are more tolerant and forgiving towards you.
Key Words: Courage, self- awareness, compassion, strength, tolerance, and forgiveness.

The Hermit

The hermit is often used to get a person out of your life, mostly a lover. The card symbolizes being alone, and starting your path alone. You can do a break up spell on yourself if you want to leave a person but cannot find the courage. However. Realize that things may escalate to a higher level to force you to decide to leave. If you do the spell on another to leave, realize that it could occur through death.
Key Words: Discretion, detachment, withdrawal, discrimination, inner wisdom, the truth at all costs, alone, and withdrawal from a relationship.

The Wheel of Fortune

The wheel of fortune is all about luck and fortune, and can be used when trying to change your situation, especially getting a job or promotion. It is often used when things are at a turning point, and you need luck, timing, and good fortune on your side. A good oil to use with this will be crown of success oil.

Key Words: Luck, timing, turning point, destiny, inevitability, a new beginning, change, and unpredictable events.

Justice

Without saying, this card is often used in court case spells, but can also be used in revenge spells to have the others get what they deserve. Justice or court case oils are normally used with this card. However. Be very careful when using this card. A person innocent according to the law and what can be proven even if they did the deed, may walk because the law says so and your spell binds the judge to abide by the letter of the law. The reverse can also happen if proof cannot be found that someone is innocent. Before asking for justice, make sure that you know the person you are doing it for is either innocent or guilty and that it can be proven. You may want to word your spell that proof must be found either way.

Key Words: Justice, fairness, harmony, cause and effect, equality, balance, responsibility, and getting what one deserves.

The Hanged Man

The hanged man is not often used in candle magic, except to get a person to change their mind about something. Normally about a relationship or job. By getting them to be bored with their relationship or job, they may leave it.

Key Words: Change, transition, readjustment, limbo, paradox, sacrifice, static relationship, boredom, change of mind, and relinquish control.

Death

Many people are afraid of the death card, but should not be. When one cycle ends, another begins. The death card is thus used with ending things. Either a relationship, a bad habit, a job, or a situation.

Be forewarned, that if you use the card in a spell, the end may be dramatic. A relationship may end in a massive fight. You may be fired from your job if asking to move jobs. You ask, and the universe creates the situations as hard as needs be to get you to move and end the current cycle. The card can be used with ending poverty or ending a curse against you, or even a string of bad luck.
Key Words: New beginnings, death, endings, transformation, parting ways, and separation.

Temperance

This card can be used to end an argument by having opposite sides find a middle ground or to have the other side compromise. Used with the lovers' card, this can smooth over relationship problems and bring back harmony to the relationship, if a love spell was not used to get the other person. Lavender oil, or love oil may be used for relationship problems, and lavender oil for problems with coworkers or family members.
Key Words: Compromise, self-control, virtues, moderation, merging of ideas, harmony, understanding, and healing.

The Devil

Using this card in spells is usually for bad. Normally for cursing another. Bad things may befall the other person. This card may be used with a reversing candle, but then you are adding to the karma that the other person will receive by punishing them extra. At times, it may be required to get another to stop attacking you. However. Think very carefully about using this card. For a powerful reversing spell, use it with the death card.
Key Words: Materialism, bondage, lies, temptation, ignorance, desire for money and power, unconscious reactions, being obsessed, addiction, manipulation, and negative thinking.

The Tower

As can be seen from the image on the card, this card is all about sudden change, normally for the worse. Thus, the card is mostly used in curse magic to turn another person's life into a living hell. Used with the devil card, things can turn very bad for another person.

However. If the spell fails, things will turn extra bad for you very fast. Like the devil card, this is not one you want to work with lightly.
Key Words: Change, unexpected events, revelation, chaos, external disruption, abandoning the old, dramatic upheaval, change in fortune, and unexpected challenges.

The Star

This card is about inspiration and guidance, and a good card to use if you feel using magic is not acceptable for self-gain. When using the card with a prosperity or business success spell, you are asking to have the motivation and guidance to change your financial situation by physical means. You may get ideas in dreams, books, from people, and so on, be open to them. Used with the lovers' card, you are asking not just for love, but ideal love. However. Be forewarned that you may fall pregnant, as a mother-child relationship is normally ideal love.
Key Words: Ideal love, inspiration, truth, success, guidance, motivation, and trust.

The Moon

The moon represents the shadow side of the sun. Although many practitioners work with the moon and the moon is concerned with wellbeing, the card represents the dark side of the night. And as such, is often used in curse magic or court cases to let the opposition be confused, blind to the truth, and losing it.
Key Words: Fear, self-deceit, intuition, affair, blind to the truth, confused, apprehension, illusion, losing touch with reality, and worry.

The Sun

This card at its core represents success and happiness, and thus can be used in any business success, prosperity, job seeking, exam, and so on spells. Even though it represents success, it should not be used in court case spells unless you are sure the person you are doing it for is totally innocent. The card should never be added to a love spell as at its core, a love spell is a controlling spell and the target of the spell may look happy with you, but their soul will be angry for being controlled and bound, which is at a difference with the sun card representing happiness.

Key Words: Sharing, communication, joy, happiness, positive energy, creative growth, self-believe, and self-confidence.

Judgment

This card like the justice card is often used in court cases. However. It can be used in any argument where the truth needs to come out so that the guilty party can be judged. Thus, if the truth is hidden it can be used that it comes out that the judge can make the right decision, either guilty or innocent. This card may be used in settling arguments or court cases with the empress card to allow the right judgment to be made as the truth comes out and that compassion is shown. If you or the person you are doing the spell for is guilty, this may be a better option than trying to control the judge to make an innocent ruling, for if that fails, the sentence will be harsher. Whereas when this one fails, you will be back to as if you have done nothing, and the ruling will be the same and not harsher.

Key Words: Judgement, liberation, transformation, acceptance, truth, and choice.

The World

The world is normally a positive card and is mostly about moving forward and change. The card can be used to help change situations, like poverty, stuck in a job or relationship, or just to allow change into your life. As the card is about travel as well, it may help you to finally get up and move to another town, city, or country. The card can also be used with a prosperity spell when you feel you are not getting your just reward. However. Be totally honest with yourself if you actually do deserve what you desire. You may think you deserve a promotion but in fact, are lazy at work and deserve to be fired.

Key Words: Freedom, completion, full circle, cosmic love, free from fear, rewards earned, travel, and awareness.

Chapter 16: Runes and Candles

Runes have been used for centuries, and are very powerful symbols to use on candles. Although each rune stands for a letter, they also represent a thought or idea. Using runes is a very easy and short way to say what you want. For instance, prosperity, protection, victory, and so on. The runes can be used with tarot cards if you wish, such as the chariot card and the victory rune, or the abundance rune with the empress or world card. Alternatively, you can carve the rune directly into the candle and place the same sign on a paper under the candle, or just use a paper under the candle with the appropriate rune on it. For added effect, runes can be combined, such as the victory rune with the abundance rune, or the victory rune with the protection rune.

Note that there are different rune alphabets and that the meanings of runes are disputed. Following are the more generally accepted descriptions of runes. The runes are divided into three groups (Aett) with eight runes per group. Each group has a different theme.

The First Aett is Freyr's Aett.

Key Words: Love, Fertility, Life Force, and Increase.

Fehu (Feoh, F)

Sacred to Freya, Goddess of fertility and love.

Key Words: Fortune, stability, security, success, protection of wealth, and wealth.

Uruz (UR, U, V)

Sacred to Thor, God of thunder and strength.

Key Words: Power, increase sexual potency, enhance energy for hunting, increase one's willpower, endings, luck, magical power boost, end old cycles, removal of self-doubt, new opportunities, power rune to boost spell energy, and creativity.

Thurisaz (Thorn, th)

A Rune sacred to Loki, trickster, and shape changer.
Key Words: Conflict, contemplation, security, protection, breakthroughs, luck, change, and dynamic defense.

Ansuz (Asa, A)

A Rune sacred to Odin, God of Wind and Spirit.
Key Words: Joy, happiness, new beginnings, harmony, order, communication, wisdom, clarity, attract others to your cause, increase magical energy, psychic power, inspiration, revealing what is hidden, memory, study, past-life regression, and Odin.

Raidho (Rad, R)

A Rune sacred to Thor and thunder.
Key Words: Protection (especially while traveling) (mark your luggage or vehicle with this rune), astral and physical travel, personal development, justice, remove blockages, and bring about change.

Kenaz (Cen, K)

A Rune sacred to Heimdall, the underworld watcher.

Key Words: Creativity, inspiration, help with study and exams, fertility, hope, dispelling anxiety and fear, reveals secrets, find hidden knowledge, and love magic.

Gebo (Gyfu, G)

A Rune of a sacred mark dedicated to the Gods.
Key Words: Generosity, kindness, aid, peace, blessed relationships, unity, luck, harmony, sex magic, and balance.

Wunjo (Wyn, W, V)

A Rune sacred to Odin.
Key Words: Gain both in material and emotions, renewed energy, comfort, change for the better, peace, balance, harmony, hope, wishes, empathy, fellowship, love, joy, very powerful wishing rune, happiness, empathy when dealing with legal matters, protect against jealousy, and prosperity.

The Second Aett is Hagal's Aett (Heimdall).
Key Words: Limitations, fate, and the inner journey.

Hagalaz (Haegl, H)

A Rune sacred to Heimdall.
Key Words: Overcoming obstacles, banishment, protection against storms and evil, wisdom, and aid in decision-making.

Naudhiz (Nyd)

A Rune sacred to Norns, weavers of fate.
Key Words: Patience, limitations, banishing, transformation, magic, war fetter, banishing evil, binding curses, turning frustration into your advantage, turning a bad situation around, helps with success in any venture, and curse breaker. Break down obstacles, bonds, holds, locks, and fetters. When things are dire, use this rune.

Isa (Isa, I)

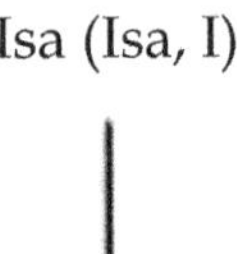

A Rune sacred to intensity.
Key Words: Blocking, cursing, freezing something, creates obstacles, creates mental blocks, ruin a relationship, bind and freeze curses, obliterate unwanted activity from another (freezing the power of the one that cursed you), and binding.

Jera (Jera, J, Y)

A Rune sacred to Freya and Frey.
Key Words: Strong success rune, abundance, generosity, improvement, gentle revolution, change, legal success, harvest what is owed to you, get what you deserve in legal matters, fertility, rewards for work done, luck, turn dreams into reality, break through stagnation when the work has already been done, and can help break locks, bonds, and curses that halts your due rewards.

Eihwaz (Eoh, I)

A Rune sacred to Odin.
Key Words: Death, new beginnings, endurance, magical protection, endings, stop self-abuse, banishing, obstacle remover, self-healing, defense. Break through bonds, holds, curses, blockages, and other stagnation.

Perthro (Peorth)

A Rune sacred to Frigg, the all mother.
Key Words: Showing what is hidden, understanding, answers, spiritual evolution, and divination. Unlock ancestral memories and gain wisdom and answers. Dream magic, meditation, and spiritual guidance.

Elhaz (Algiz)

A Rune sacred to Heimdall.
Key Words: Protection, assistance in defense, luck, and to give shelter. Protect your home and belongings (draw the rune on your baggage when traveling). Similar to the Fatima, being a hand to ward off evil. Increases magical power. Protects your job when rivals are around. Wear a talisman with this rune to create a protective shield around you.

Sowilo (Sol)

A Rune sacred to Balder.

Key Words: Wealth, health, happiness, spiritual enlightenment, creativity, guidance, strengthen of magical will, healing, victory, success, and self-confidence. Use when times are hard and much needs to be done to gain victory.

The Third Aett is Tyr's Aett

Key Words: Synthesis, integration, and connection with the spirit and others.

Tiwaz (Tyr)

A Rune sacred to Tyr.
Key Words: Bravery, steadfastness, self-confidence, passion, energy, victory, faith, knowledge, success, healing, justice, war, honor, confidence during a battle, steadfastness against any adversary, success and victory in any contest, legal matters (cannot be used to pervert justice), and increase finances honorably.

Berkano (Beorc)

A Rune sacred to the Earth Goddess.
Key Words: Healing, making a fresh start, achieving conception, new beginnings, new projects, protection (especially young children and teenage girls), and prosperity.

Ehwaz (Eh)

A Rune sacred to Frey.
Key Words: Travel, swift change, sex binding, remover of obstacles in marriage, protection, astral travel, brings people to your cause, and luck.

Mannaz (Man)

A Rune sacred to Odin and Heimdall.
Key Words: Intelligence, success in study, use when help is needed from others, psychic harmony, teamwork, and cooperation.

Laguz (Lagus)

A Rune sacred to Njord.
Key Words: Magical powers, psychic ability, confidence in oneself, clairvoyance, success in studies, gives access to dreams, creativity, vitality, and passion (especially for women).

Ingwaz (Ing)

A Rune sacred to Frey.
Key Words: Peace, prosperity, fertility, powerful sex magic, enhances potential, completion of projects, obstacle remover, and protection (especially home and workplace).

Dagaz (Dag)

A Rune sacred to Heimdall.
Key Words: Completion, balance, endings, bring a positive outcome to a situation, clarity, success, abundance, banish negativity, opens doors and paths on all planes and removes obstacles, money, luck (when worn), and harmony.

Othala (Odal)

A Rune sacred to heritage.
Key Words: Strong rune for protection of, material possessions (especially inheritance), family values, and freedom. It enhances peace, security and prosperity, travel (breaks bonds from traditional values or clans to allow freedom to travel), and fortune.

Chapter 17: Sigils and Candles

Sigil of Archangel-Michael.

This chapter serves as an introduction to a fascinating, but potentially complex subject. Sigils are used in both low and high magic and are some of the oldest magic around. It is believed that by using the correct sigil, your spell is almost guaranteed to work. In essence, a sigil is a form of shorthand writing for spells, as well as identifying entities, such as a sigil for angels. In other words, a sigil is a symbol that is created for a specific spell. You can draw from a large number of sigils readily available that are easy to find with a quick search on the internet, or you can make your own. If you are new to magic, consider standard sigils already used.

Note that as with all magic, sigil magic is just as if you wrote your spell on the candle or paper normally, thus intent and wording are key. Forget to include something, and your spell may not work, or not as you intended.

The thought behind using a sigil is that your conscious mind gets in the way by being distracted by everyday things. However. A symbol or pattern can easily be programmed into your subconscious mind. When a specific idea is associated with the symbol or pattern, your subconscious mind will remember it every time you see it. Thus, you could create a sigil for anything, from helping you study, to running your own successful business. The sigil can be as simple or as complicated as you like.

There are several different ways to create a sigil, and this is where the subject can get very interesting and also complicated, depending on you. Experiment, and get a way that works for you.

A common method used to create a sigil is to use kameas (magic squares). If calling an entity, its name would be converted into numbers and traced on the squares, creating a pattern. You can do this for a spell as well. However. To convert every letter in a spell to a number would create a very complex sigil. To make the sigil simpler, various letters are removed by different methods.

One method is to write out your intent (spell), then remove all the vowels (A, E, I, O, U), next, remove all the repeated letters. You will now have a weird-sounding glyph. You can draw the letters into a symbol, or you can use the Hebrew letter to number table to convert the letters to numbers and a pattern.

1	2	3	4	5	6	7	8
A	B	C	D	E	U	O	F
I	K	G	M	H	V	Z	P
Q	R	L	T	N	W		
J		S			X		
Y							

For example, let's take PROTECTION FROM ALL EVIL.
If we remove the vowels, we get, PRTCTNFRMLLVL.
If we remove the duplicate letters, we get PRTCNFMLV.
Using the Hebrew Numerological system, we get.

1	2	3	4	5	6	7	8
A	B	C	D	E	U	O	F
I	K	G	M	H	V	Z	P
Q	R	L	T	N	W		
J		S			X		
Y							

Now all you have to do is learn the strokes like a signature. You can also shorten it to just PROTECTION, which will come out as, PRTCN, or:

1	2	3	4	5	6	7	8
A	B	C	D	E	U	O	F
I	K	G	M	H	V	Z	P
Q	R	L	T	N	W		
J		S			X		
Y							

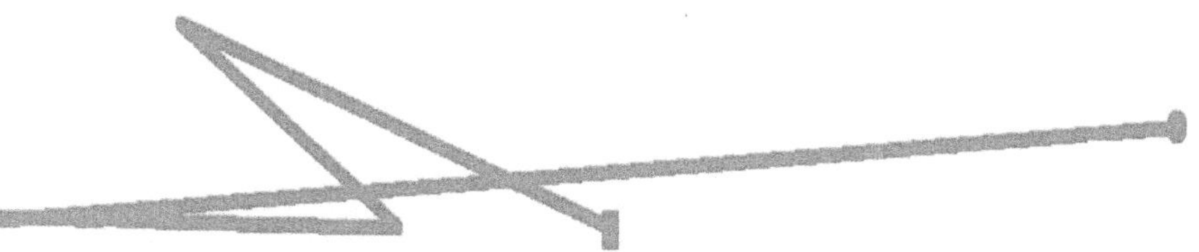

You can now add the protection sigil to your protection candle.

Note, for very long spells, you can use the first letter of every word, then remove the vowels and duplicate letters, as you wish. What counts is that when you are done, the sigil has meaning to you. It should be noted that this use is different from some that say to plant the sigil in your mind and forget it, as this way we will keep remembering our sigil and actually let our subconscious mind send energy towards our goal every time we see or use the sigil. When we use words, it is thought that the conscious mind can cloud things with doubt. This does not happen with sigils.

Chapter 18: Power Symbols

There are a large number of power symbols that have been used over centuries, with many taking on different meanings as different religions used it for their purpose. Following are several symbols you can use on your candles to add additional power. Remember, as with all magic, intent and belief are key. If a symbol does not feel right to you, do not use it as it may affect your spell negatively or in ways you did not expect.

The Moon

The moon glows with the reflective light of the sun and gives light in the darkness when nothing else does. It is linked to the feminine Devine energy, and allows one to connect to the cosmic magical energy (drawing down the moon). If you work with the moon, drawing the moon on your candle can add additional energy to it. There are three generally recognized moon symbols, representing the Maiden, Mother, and Crone, called the triple moon or goddess. You can draw one symbol only or all three together if you wish. Shown, is a triple goddess symbol with a pentacle in the middle.
Key Words: Protection, rebirth, making a fresh start, giving light in darkness, psychic perception, and magic.

The Hamsa

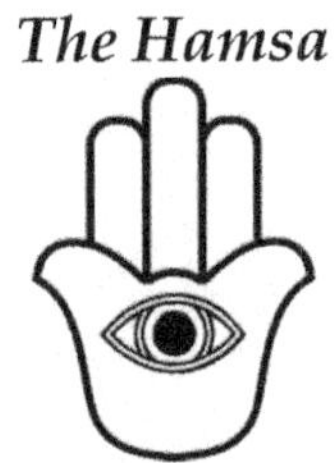

The Hamsa is a symbol of the open palm of a human hand, often with the Nazar (eye) in the middle. The symbol is very popular in the Middle East and North Africa. Its exact origin is unknown, but it is thought to have originated in Ancient Egypt or Carthage (modern-day Tunisia).

The Hamsa is thought to possibly have been associated with the goddess Tanit.
Key Words: Protection, especially against the evil eye or jealousy.

They Eye of Horus (Wadjet)

Horus was the son of Osiris and Isis, Egyptian Gods. He was called, 'Horus who rules with two yes.' His right eye was white and represented the sun, while his left eye was black and represented the moon and the god Djehuti (Thoth). In a battle against Seth who had murdered Osiris, Horus lost his left eye. Horus's eye was later recovered, and he offered it to his father, Osiris, who was then resurrected as a god in the underworld.
Key Words: Protection (especially from jealousy), restoration, rebirth, wisdom, see what is hidden, truth, and starting anew.

Key

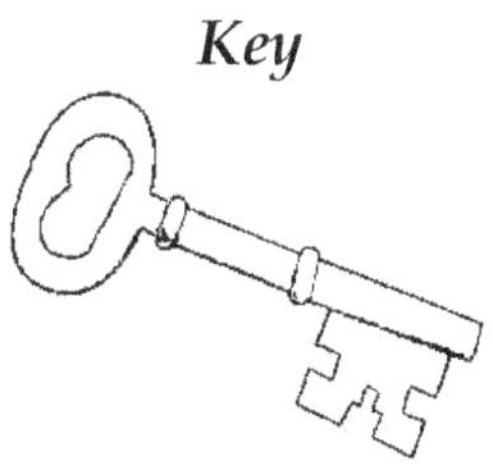

Although keys both lock and unlock things, they are traditionally more used to unlock and clear obstacles, as well as create new possibilities. This is a great symbol to use with the fortune rune or any other wealth rune. Good for any change needed. Can be used in curse magic to lock opportunities, paths, money flow, and so on. Traditionally, the old form (pictured before) of a key is used.
Key Words: Unlocking or locking opportunity, removing or creating obstacles, revealing what is hidden or hiding something, unlocking new possibilities or ideas.

Pentacle

The pentacle is one of the oldest symbols around, and originally had no negative meaning when turned around. The negative meaning is a modern creation. The pentacle has been found in artifacts all over the world, and predates many other symbols. Traditionally, the five points resembled that of the five metaphysical elements of the ancients. When a circle is drawn around the pentacle, it represents the God-Goddess, and adds to the power of the pentacle.

Spirit: The top corner. Represents the all and the Devine.
Earth: The lower left hand corner. Represents stability and physical endurance.
Fire: The lower right hand corner. Represents courage and daring.
Water: Upper right hand corner. Represents emotions and intuition.
Air: Upper left hand corner. Represents intelligence and the arts.
Key Words: Protection, universal wisdom, reflection, abundance, and magic.

Hexagram / Star of David

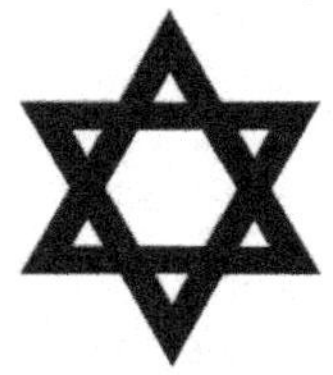

The Magen David, also known as the Jewish Star or Star of David, has been in use for centuries and predates Christianity. The star is used in many religions, including Jewish, Hinduism, and occultism. The hexagon consists of two triangles. One pointed up and the other down; locked in a harmonious embrace. The downward-pointing triangle represents Shakti and is the sacred embodiment of femininity, while the upward-pointing triangle represents Shiva and is the sacred embodiment of masculinity. The hexagon is also referred to as the Seal of Solomon, and is often used in high magic to call or banish demons and other entities.

Although the Magen David is generally recognized as a Jewish religious symbol, it was only adopted as a Jewish religious symbol in the Middle Ages. The symbol however was used by other religions as a religious symbol far earlier.

The Hexagram is seen as a combination of the four elements. Fire is represented by the upwards pointing triangle: Air is also an upwards pointing triangle, but has a horizontal line through its center. Water is represented by a downwards pointing triangle, while Earth is a downwards pointing triangle, but with a horizontal line through its center.
Key Words: Protection, balance, magic, calling up spirits, hex breaking, and curse-breaking.

Menorah

The menorah is an ancient Hebrew seven-lamp (six branches), or nine-lamp stand, originally made from pure gold. According to legend, it was used in the portable sanctuary Moses used, and then 300 years later in the Temple in Jerusalem. It has been used as a Jewish symbol since ancient times, and is currently the emblem on the coat of arms of Israel.
Key Words: Wisdom, and universal enlightenment.

Maltese Cross

The Maltese cross is associated with Christianity, and identified with the Knights Hospitaller (Knights of Malta), that are Christian warriors. The eight points of the cross represent the eight chivalric virtues listed in italic. The cross is used in various organizations, such as fire and rescue badges.
Key Words: Order, loyalty, piety, frankness, bravery, glory, honor, acceptance of death, respect, protection, and compassion.

Yin-Yang

The Yin-Yang represents the completeness of the universe, combining the two contradictory forces of nature. The outer circle represents everything, while the Yin represents female energy that stands for negative, darkness, softness, moisture, night-time, and even numbers. The Yang represents male energy that stands for positive, brightness, hardness, dryness, daytime, and odd numbers. It is seen that as the one energy moves, so does the other, both trying to be in a state of balance. If you are going through a bad time and need some harmony and balance in your life, this is a good symbol to use.
Key Words: Balance, natural and universal laws, and healing.

Ohm

The ohm is a deeply spiritual symbol, often seen on Buddhist objects. Traditionally, each curve of the symbol has its own meaning.

The larger lower curve represents the waking world.
The upper left curve represents a state of deep sleep.
The open semi-circle at the top represents the infinite, which is linked to the state of absolute consciousness, called the Turiya.
Key Words: Spirituality, spiritual growth, harmony, and balance.

Bagua

In Chinese, Ba means eight, and Gua means trigram. The Bagua consists of eight sacred elements, which are sometimes called the Trigrams. The symbol is said to have been inscribed on the back of a turtle that rose from the Yellow River at the dawn of time, and that the secrets of the universe are contained within the symbol. The symbol is used to encourage one's life force (chi) to flow, which will enhance all aspects of spirituality as well as life. When you feel drained, stuck in a rut, depressed, need inspiration, try this symbol with a healing candle.
Key Words: Chi, secrets, knowledge, and spiritual growth. The Yin-Yang is often displayed in the middle.

Celtic Knot

The Celtic knot symbolizes the flow of the life force that runs through the universe and all of us. It represents your fate, from birth to death, and your karma. The symbol is often used to change your karma, or destiny. It can be used to change any situation you are in, such as a bad relationship, poverty, down on luck, and so forth. Combine the symbol with the appropriate symbol you want change in. For instance, combine this with the remover of obstacles and fortune rune to create a powerful spell. Know that there are several different ways to draw the symbol, each with a slightly different meaning.
Key Words: Universe, life force (chi), life, birth, death, rebirth, destiny, and karma.

Ankh

The ankh is seen as the original cross and predates Christianity. It is a very powerful protection symbol and has been found in artifacts all over the world. The symbol represents both physical and eternal life. It is believed that the Ankh creates a connection with the divine or universe energy, and that the wearer can absorb the energy, which will give protection, better health, and spiritual power to the wearer.
Key Words: Protection (especially against evil and decay), healing, and life energy.

Nazar/ Evil Eye

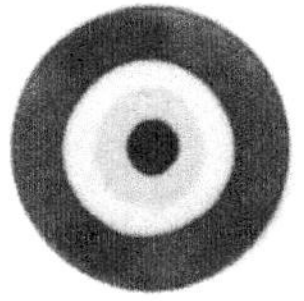

Greeks and Turks have used the Nazar for centuries to protect the wearer from the karma and negativity send by jealous and envious people that wish them harm. This is a very good symbol to use if things start to go wrong and no curse is detected, or when you know someone has a knife ready to stab you in the back. Also a good symbol to use for a monthly protection spell, especially if you are going up in the world. Know that sometimes your best friends and family may be secretly sending negative and hateful thoughts, even if they celebrate your success.
Key Words: Protection, especially from envy and jealousy.

Win in Court Amulet

This symbol can be worn as an amulet. It has no known origin and is made up of several different symbols. It is said to enhance the wearer's charisma and ability to gain sympathy in all legal matters, especially when appearing in front of judges.
Key Words: Victory in legal battles.

Norse Spell Charm

This symbol is the Nordic version of the Nazar, and is used to protect against the karma, and negative energy sent by others that are jealous of you and envy your status. It can be used exactly as the Nazar.
Key Words: Protection against envy, jealousy, evil, and negativity.

Valknut (Odin's Knot)

The Valkut is seen as a binding contract between Odin and his acolytes. It is seen as a symbol for Nordic magic, as well as knowledge. It is believed that one can change your fate or karma with the use of the symbol and is thus used with prosperity, love, and luck spells, as well as curse breaking. It should be noted that the symbol grants the user the knowledge of how to change their fate, and not do it for them. It should also be noted that as with Odin, he was granted the knowledge to change his fate, but at a high price as he lost one eye. Thus, do not expect things to change on their own with no sacrifice from your (normally hard work) when using this symbol.
Key Words: Norse magic, binding with Odin, fate, and karma.

Thor's Hammer (Mjollnir)

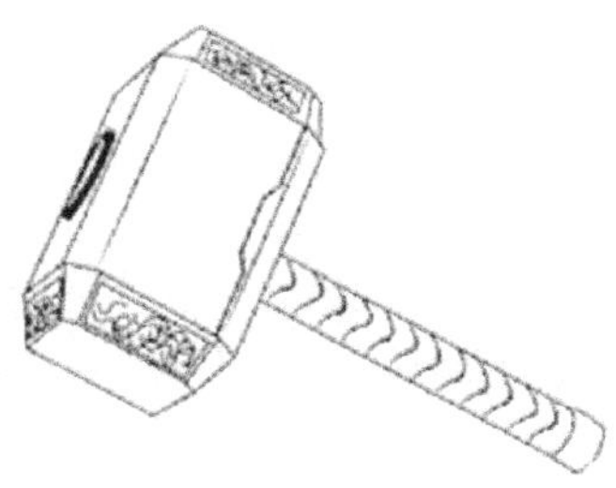

Thor's hammer is a very powerful symbol to use and can be worn as an amulet. As Thor is seen as the protector of people and crops, the hammer is often used in protection and prosperity spells, especially to protect incoming funds (crops being harvested). It can also be used against those that wish you harm, by striking them with Thor's hammer. I once had consistent bad luck, and attached a small skull and Thor's hammer to my keychain. The skull represented my enemies, and Thor's hammer would strike them continuously on the head as the keys moved, as long as they wished harm to me. Soon my troubles disappeared, without me knowing who the perpetrator was. Months later, I learned that another practitioner had complained to a friend of getting terrible headaches as if struck by a massive hammer all day, the exact same time as I put the objects on my keychain. It stopped when she decided to give up magic, interestingly the same time the skull fell of the keychain.
Key Words: Power, protection, strength, honor, and victory in battle.

Norse Pride Talisman

This is a very powerful symbol to use, although a bit hard to engrave on a candle. The symbol features Thor's head inside his hammer, with Thor's beard twirling into a Celtic Knot. This symbol basically combines the three symbols to form a symbol that is more powerful than each symbol on its own. Change your fate and knock down obstacles and adversaries with this symbol.
Key Words: Eternal protection, strength, power, and change fate.

Chapter 19: Crystals and Candles

Crystals have been used on their own and with candles as part of magical rituals for centuries. Crystals give off a unique vibration that affects the energy around them, and exact change in humans working with them. You can use this to enhance your candle spells, or you can charge a crystal with a candle spell and then wear it on your body.

There is a vast number of options to choose from when it comes to crystals, as well as how to use them. Find what works best for you and ask your local crystal shop for advice.

To start with, try placing a crystal that has the same properties as your spell, next to the candleholder to amplify your spell. You can charge the crystal beforehand with the same intent as the spell you are going to do, say for instance, prosperity. Alternatively, as the candle burns, hold the crystal and imagine how the power of the spell flows into the crystal and charges it. Imagine how the crystal forms an aura around you and changes the energy around you towards your purpose. Say for instance, making you look more trustworthy in a job application or court case, or attracting wealth by customers wanting to buy from you. If you charge the crystal with a spell, wear it on your person, either as a pendant, bracelet, or in your handbag.

To add additional power to your spells, you can form a crystal grid around the spell candle. This can be in the form of any of the runes, power symbols, sigils, or a host of layouts available on the internet. For instance, you can use the layout of the Fehu rune with crystals for prosperity, such as citrine, jade, diamond, and so on, around an abundance candle.

Following is a list of the more popular crystals to help you get started. Ask your crystal shop for help in choosing the right crystals for the spell you wish to do.

Attract Abundance: Citrine, jade, lapis lazuli, ruby, aventurine, bloodstone, diamond, emerald, malachite, tourmaline, jasper, and sapphire.
Attract Love: Rose quartz, kunzite, malachite, aquamarine, sapphire, and jade.
Astral Travel: Citrine, honey calcite, amethyst, and diamond.
Banishing: Selenite, citrine, obsidian, and smokey quartz.
Cleanse Self: Selenite, and rose quartz.
Cleanse an Area: Obsidian, selenite, rose quartz, clear quartz, and amethyst.
Creativity: Garnet.
Healing: Rose quartz, calcite, dolomite, clear quartz, amethyst, bloodstone, and carnelian.
Judgment: Aventurine.
Material Goals: Jade, jet, and ruby.
Meditation: Amethyst, azurite, fluorite, and jade.
Positive Mood: Citrine, rose quartz, calcite, dolomite, amber, amethyst, goldstone, agate, and lapis lazuli.
Protection Magical: Black tourmaline, sapphire, ruby, blue coral, obsidian, black onyx, smokey quartz, amber, carnelian, hematite, and tiger's eye.
Protection Physical Harm: Malachite, ruby, hematite, and tiger's eye.
Protection for Travel: Jade, and malachite.
Protect Money: Citrine, jade, lapis lazuli, and ruby.
Success: Amazonite.
New Opportunities: Lapis lazuli, and jade.
Past-Life Connection: Obsidian, ruby, fossils, and jasper.

Chapter 20: Paper and Candle Spells

Writing your wish on a piece of paper, leaf, or tree bark, and then burning it, is one of the oldest magical practices. Before candles became widespread commercially available, this was very common. However. Since many people could not write, often, sigils, runes, or symbols were used to convey the message they wanted.

Using a candle with a paper spell combines the two methods, to give added power. You can still write your spell on the candle as well as carve any sigils, runes, or symbols you want into the candle, just as you are writing it on paper. Just make sure that if you write a spell on the candle and paper, that they match word-for-word.

Once you have written your spell on a paper, either read it out aloud or for yourself three times, then fold it two to three times. You can either put the paper under the candle, or you can light the paper with the flame of the candle. If you put the paper under the candle, burn it when the candle is done. If you have no candle, you can fold your paper up, and place an appropriate crystal on top of the paper and leave it on your altar until you feel it is time, then burn the paper. The paper is an instant spell, while the candle is a longer spell with more power. Paper is good for instant results with few obstacles. Candles have more power to break through obstacles but may take longer. For less powerful and slower, but longer-lasting spells, consider using a witch bottle or crystal grid. These are good for overall protection and abundance spells.

Warning, never wrap the paper around the candle, not even if it is wax or parchment paper. The paper will catch fire when the candle has burned down enough, and may cause the wax to melt away, or could even cause a massive fire.

If you want to add more power to the spell, use color paper that matches your spell. You can also lightly apply a bit of oil that corresponds to your spell, onto the paper. You can also sprinkle a small amount of dried herbs or powder onto the paper before you fold it. Burn the paper on its own as a spell or when the candle is done if you placed it under the candle.

Do be careful when burning the paper, as you may burn yourself. A good idea is to place the paper into a fireproof container. You can use a disposable foil baking holder used to bake small loaves of bread and available from many stores, to burn your paper in. Make sure that the paper burns completely to ash. If a piece remains, fear not, as it often happens when not enough air gets to the paper when folded. Just relight the peace with the candle flame or what you used to light the candle (you can hold the piece with tweezers). When the paper has completely burned to ash, scatter the ash to the winds. Whatever ash remains in the holder, you can wash it away with water and give it to earth. This way, both heaven and earth received your request. Just never flush the ash down the toilet.

For added power, write your words in color ink that corresponds to the spell you are doing. Alternatively, use dragon's blood ink in a refillable calligraphy pen for general spells and protection, dove's blood ink for love spells, and war water or four thieves vinegar for banishing and curse-breaking. For stopping nasty curses against you, use shut the fuck up oil.

Chapter 21: Spells To Get You Started

Although there are thousands upon thousands of spells to be found in books, on the internet, and from other practitioners, most claiming to be the one to do, you should always opt for the spell that feels right to you. When anointing candles, choose the method that feels right to you, from the ones described in chapter 7, step 10.

Following are several simple spells and rituals to get you started. Use them as-is, or modify them to your liking. Note, as I do not have control over how the spells are used, I take no karma or responsibility from your actions. As well, as I do not believe in doing love, cursing, or binding spells when you are starting out, doing them usually causes more harm than good, thus those spells are not included within this book.

Protection Spells

There are a large number of protection spells on the market, some very basic, some very complex. Following are a mix of different protection spells that have ingredients that are relatively easy to find.

Essential Oil Protection (Also Banishing and Hex Breaking)

One of the simplest antidote or protection spells is to throw three drops of rosemary oil and a teaspoon or two of coarse salt (or Epson salt) into your bathwater and soak for half an hour. This is normally effective enough to break most hexes, curses, jinxes, and keeps anyone from putting one onto you. The salt should also drain away all negativity around you. A teaspoon of dried rosemary herbs from your spice rack and table salt can be used in a pinch.

Single White or Blue Candle Protection

A very easy protection spell is to take a white or blue candle, anoint it with protection oil (white sage, sandalwood, frankincense, dragon's blood, or a special mix), inscribe the word protection on it, as well as a protection sigil, or use one of the runes or power symbols. When you charge the candle, imagine it dispels all negativity and darkness around you, and that it makes a protective bubble the same as the candle color around you (blue is traditionally seen as the strongest protection color).

If you need to be discreet, use tea light candles. Remove them from the holder, anoint and charge them, then return them to the holder. No one will know you are doing a spell, and they can be left burning if you should go to bed provided you make sure they cannot set anything alight. Best to place them in a bowl or plate with water around them.

Multi Candle Protection

For this spell, you will need four or eight white candles and a blue candle. Write protection on the blue candle and use runes or symbols describing protection if you wish. Write banishing on the white candles and use runes or symbols for banishing evil and negativity. Place four or eight white candles around the blue candle. Light the blue candle, then the white candles going in a clockwise direction. Imagine the white candles banishing all evil and negativity from you and your life as well as making an impenetrable white bubble around you. All negativity that tries to reach you is instantly vaporized. Imagine the blue candle making a blue inner protection bubble around you.

Mirror Protection

Another effective protection spell is to take a mirror, hold it in front of you with the reflection away from you. Now turn anti-clockwise while saying. Circle of reflection, circle of protection, may the sender of all harm, feel the power of this charm. Do this three times as in three complete circles where you say the rhyme once on each circle. Finish with, so be it. This spell can be done once a day or month as you feel the need.

Banishing Spells

Traditionally, banishing spells use black and or white candles. However. You can use different colors depending on your needs.

Toilet Paper Banish

This is a very easy but effective spell that works well to get someone out of your life. Write what or whom you want to be banished from your life on a piece of toilet paper.

Say that you are banishing the person or the situation (poverty or bad luck, for instance) from your life, and imagine how the person or situation leaves you. Now throw the toilet paper in the toiler, and flush it away while imagining your problems being flushed away.

Single Candle Banishing

A very easy banishing spell is to take a black candle, anoint it with banishing oil (sage or frankincense will do as well). Write banish on the candle as well as using any runes or symbols that represent banishing that you feel comfortable in using. Imagine all evil and bad luck or whatever you want to be banished, being blown away from you forever, never to return.

Two Candles Banishing

Anoint a black candle as described in the single candle banishing spell, and then anoint either a white candle or a color candle in the color of what you want back in your life. The white or color candle will be anointed with oils and herbs as well as symbols of what you want. Say for instance, you are banishing poverty, and then you may use a green candle with patchouli or cinnamon or money oil. Light the black candle as with the single candle spell. Just before the black candle burns out, light the white or color candle with the flame of the black candle, and then imagine how what you want in your life comes back to you. It is okay if the black candle burns a bit still while the color candle burns.

You can use the banishing powder listed below on its own or with a banishing candle spell. If you want to use it with a candle, either use castor oil to make a banishing oil to anoint the candles, or burn them on a charcoal block next to the candle. You can also sprinkle the powder as is on the clothes (especially shoes) of the person you want gone (be sparing so no trace is visible), or you can sprinkle the powder in the path the person takes. Sprinkling the powder in the person's path works very well if you do not know who is exactly working against you, but know where they shop (do it at the doors of all spell and candle shops around the area).

Be Gone Powder

Mix black pepper, cayenne pepper, sea salt, chopped bay laurel leaves, sulfur, and powdered hydrangea blossoms (if you can find them or use cinnamon).

Change or Be Gone

This spell does give the person an option of changing or leaving your life.

Mix patchouli, vetiver, castor, and olive oil. Discreetly (very lightly) rub this on the doorknobs of the person's home or door handles of his or her car, alternatively, their house or car keys.

Cleansing Spells

Cleansing should be done before you begin with spell work, and at least once a month. It is not needed to go overboard every time you do spells or even every month. However. You should at least do a thorough cleansing once a year or every six months if possible. Remember, as you do spells, you naturally attract dark entities that feed of your energy. They may cause spells to be weakened to the point that the spells fail.

Mind Cleansing

A very easy and effective cleansing method is just to sit down and imagine how you fill the room with white light and dispel all negativity. You can then imagine a blue light filling the room and providing protection.

Incense Stick Cleansing

Light an incense stick of either space clearing, or a fragrance such as white sage, frankincense, dragons' blood, rosemary or sandalwood, to clear an area. For a powerful mix, mix dragon's blood with white sage and rosemary oil (or granules or powder) and burn on a charcoal block or oil diffuser.

Salt Water Spray
Mix pure coarse sea salt with spring or rainwater (bottled spring water is fine). Pour into a mist sprayer (one used to water ferns and other plants) and then lightly mist the area to be cleaned. You can add rose oil or rose petals if you wish and add an amethyst crystal to the bottle.

Candle Blessing and Clearing
Dress a white and blue candle with blessing or clearing oil, and burn to clear an area.

Mix frankincense and benzoin essential oil with olive and jojoba oil and anoint the candles. You can add rosemary if you want, or substitute it for the frankincense oil if you do not have it. You can burn these candles next to your bath while taking a bath for a powerful self-cleanser. Add rosemary oil (three to nine drops) as well as a bit of Epson salt (or coarse sea salt if you cannot find Epson salt) to the bathwater. Use small candles such as birthday candles or candles burning around 30 minutes or so. Stay in the bath until the candles are burned out, and then drain the water while laying down in the bath. Imagine all negativity leaving you and being sucked down the drain.

Better Business / Prosperity Spells

Better business spells normally not only attract customers but also make them spend money as well as protect against theft.

Basil Spell 1
Write prosperity on a dried basil leaf in silver or gold ink and then burn the leaf while imagining prosperity entering your life. You can do this with a prosperity candle spell by using the flame of the candle to light the leaf.

Basil Spell 2
Take a half-cup of fresh basil leaves and cover with about 500ml of boiling spring or rain water (bottled non-sparkling spring water is fine). Let the mixture stand for three days. Strain the mixture and use the basil-scented water as a floor wash in your business. Sprinkle some (gently) at the corners of your business, on the doorstep, behind tills, and behind doors.

You may also use it as a cleaner and wipe your counters down as well as your cash register. If you work only from a laptop or computer or other mobile devices, wipe them down with a damp cloth with this mixture.

You can use basil essential oil and mix it with spring or rainwater to the same effect, but it is more expensive. You can also add a few drops of basil oil to your bath water to attract wealth and make better business. Patchouli oil added strengthens the mixture.

Bend Over or Compelling Oil

If you are going for a job interview or business deal or are a salesperson, rub bend over oil on your hands before going out for the day or meeting clients.

If you cannot find these oils, mix calamus and licorice oil with vetiver (optional) and bergamot (optional for finances but do not use on exposed skin in the sun), then add castor and jojaba oil.

Simple Candle Spell

Anoint a green candle with basil and bergamot oil. Carve the amount of money you want (or job position at the company you want to work for) in the candle as well as any symbols you want, such as remove obstacle's rune. Burn the candle completely, or if you wish 15 minutes each day until the candle is done.

Enhanced Candle Spell

Prepare a candle as the simple candle spell. Write the same message and symbols as on the candle on a piece of brown or green paper (white is fine too), then fold it and place it under the candle. When the candle is done, burn the paper and scatter the ashes to the wind or throw it in a river.

You can add coins to the spell by arranging them around the base of the candle (Chinese money coins with a square in the middle works best). You can chant a rhyme, such as money money money, come to me in abundance three times three, harm none on its path, so be it.

Curse, Hexes, and Jinx Breaking Spells

The easiest yet a powerful spell for breaking curses, bad luck, hexes, and jinxes is the Essential Oil Protection spell under protection spells.

Single Candle Spell

Take a black candle and anoint it with curse-breaking oil (sandalwood will do), then carve any symbols into the candle (the Hagalaz and Naudhiz runes are best). Place the candle in a candleholder and then place a mirror under the candle. The mirror is to strengthen the spell not reflect it back to the person that cursed you. You can reuse the mirror. Imagine how all bonds, holds, locks, and bindings around you are shattered and locked doors in front of you are blasted open. Let the candle burn down.

If you do not have time to wait, you can place the candle in a glass bowl (or cauldron), and fill it with water to just under any symbols you made (only make symbols to an inch or two below the wick, all symbols must be melted away). Let the candle burn and imagine the same as before, but when the flame hits the water, imagine how your spell is done and the water washing away all negativity from your life and all curses broken.

Iron Curse Breaker

Iron is often used in curses, as it is included in making war water. This spell breaks any curse or hex made with iron. Take three rings made of iron (hardware stores sell them) and place them in a glass of spring water (bottled spring water at the source will do), then leave it for 24 hours. The rings may rust a little, and it is the iron you want. Drink the water and imagine how the iron and water together break the curse (do not swallow the rings). You may use three iron nails instead of the rings, what you are after is the iron. Be sure to first wash the objects before placing them in a glass to remove all dirt and bacteria.

You can enhance the spell by covering the glass with white cotton or linen and expose it to the light of a full moon. Drink the water the first thing the next morning before eating or drinking anything else.

Bath and Candle Spell

Take Angelica root (can be powder) and add boiling water to it. Let it stand overnight, then drain the water off. Alternatively use angelica root essential oil. Add this and a few drops (3 to 9) of both or either sandalwood and rosemary to your bathwater. While bathing, burn a small candle (white or blue) as described in the Single White or Blue Candle Protection Spell under the Protection Spells section.

Uncrossing Spells

Unlike breaking spells that only focus on breaking the curse, uncrossing spells try to reverse the bad that has been done to your life. Thus, instead of just breaking the curse and then waiting for things to get better, you are fast-tracking your success. This is seen as a better option than a reversing spell as you do not need to break through the protection of the person that cursed you. Also, they will normally not know that you broke the curse so will not redo it. If the curse is redone, either someone around you is responsible and heard or saw things are going better, or someone hates you so much that they constantly use divination to see if you broke the curse.

Simple Candle Spell

Take a black candle and anoint it with uncrossing or van van oil. Add any symbols you wish (the Hagalaz and Naudhiz runes are best). Place the candle in a holder and then place a mirror under the holder to amplify the spell. Imagine how the spells are broken and all holds and bindings are shattered and closed doors blasted open, then imagine how your fortune returns and how things go back to how it was before your luck was changed, and you cursed.

Double Candle Spell

Make a black candle as the spell before, but add to this a white candle that is anointed with Crown of Success oil. Add the Fehu rune to the candle if you wish, or any other symbol that you associate with money and prosperity.

Light the black candle and let it almost burn out. Just before it does, light the white candle with the flame of the black candle.

Reversing Spells

Reversing spells do the same as uncrossing spells, with the addition of sending it back to the person that cursed you. However. You will need to break through their protection, and they may retaliate with even more curses, especially if it was a person hired to do the spell and not the one that hates you. For they are used to being attacked. For this reason, Uncrossing spells are seen as the best thing to do unless the attacks do not want to stop even when you break or uncross the curses.

To all the reversing spells, you can chant the following or make up a chant that you like.

Spells and magic that have been placed on me be gone (repeat three times). Go back from where you came and remain with whom you came from.

Now, visualize a white outer bubble going around you and then a blue inner bubble going around you.

Continue the chant.
I am under universal light and universal protection, and no evil can touch or harm me. So be it.

Simple Candle Spell

Take a black candle and cut the wick part off. Now turn the candle around and cut a new wick on the other end (bottom end). Basically, you will be reversing the candle. Anoint the candle with reversing oil, and carve any symbols you want into the candle to add power and reverse the spell (the Hagalaz and Naudhiz runes are best). Place the candle in a holder and then on a mirror. However. Now imagine that the mirror reflects the curse back to the person that sent it to you. If you want to add a bit of power, use a parabolic enhancing mirror (often sold at chemists), that magnifies things 10 times. You can reuse the mirror or discard it with the leftover wax when done.

To add power to this spell, do a protection spell afterward and take a bath in protection herbs or oils such as rosemary.

If you need more power to this spell or any other reversing spell, substitute the reversing oil with a mixture of War Water, Four Fingers Vinegar, and Dragon's blood oil or powder.

Double Color Candle / Multiple Candle

Get a double-color candle that is colored black outside and red inside, or black on the top and red on the bottom. Alternatively, get a red and black candle. Prepare the black candle as described before, and then anoint the red candle with van van oil to attract good to you. As before, light the black candle in a holder with a mirror under it and imagine how the bad and evil flees you and goes back to its sender. If you are using one candle, then anoint only the black part with reversing oil and the red part with van van oil. If using two candles, light the second candle with the flame of the black candle just before it dies. You can have a mirror under the red candle as well to intensify your spell. You can substitute the van van oil with crown of success oil if you cannot find van van oil, or use lemongrass oil or herbs.

Note, if you are using two candles, then turn the black candle around and cut a new wick as described in the Simple Candle Spell.

Beans Away Spell

This spell is very useful when you cannot light candles or are traveling or when the attack is ongoing.

Take a plastic fizzy drink bottle such as a Cocoa Cola bottle. Do not use normal water bottles, as the bottle needs to be able to withstand pressure, only use fizzy drink plastic bottles. Add a handful of red kidney beans to the bottle. Cover the kidney beans with freshly squeezed lemon juice (in a pinch, you can use 100% pure concentrate lemon juice available in grocery stores). The lemon juice must cover the beans when the bottle is lying flat. Imagine how all the evil sent to you, and all the evil spells and wishes and harm sent to you is trapped inside the bottle in the beans and neutralized by the lemon juice. Now secure the cap and place the bottle under your bed.

After seven days (or when you check out of your hotel if shorter than seven days), take the bottle outside. Remove the cap and throw the contents over your shoulder (any shoulder is fine). Be careful not to get some on you as it may stink. Walk away without looking at the beans. It helps if you do it in a field or bush. Discard the bottle properly (in the trash). Take a protection bath after you discarded the bottle. Keep this once-a-week ritual up for a month after things improved.

To this, you can add any protection candle spells, as well as any reversing candle spells if the curses are very strong.

Melting Weight Loss Spell

This spell will not miraculously make you lose weight overnight, but it will assist you in making lifestyle changes to allow you to lose weight.

Take a brown candle and carve your current weight at the top. Now carve your desired (realistic) weight at the bottom. Write on a piece of paper or the candle, "May I healthily and without harm to me lose weight." Be sure to add this, you do not want to get sick and end up in a hospital or get a terminal illness or lose a limb to lose weight.

Burn the candle for 10 to 15 minutes a day until the candle is done.

Happiness Candle Spell

If you are down and need some uplifting and warmth, this spell may help. Take an orange candle and anoint it with lavender oil. Burn the candle while holding the palms of your hands around the flame at a safe distance. Imagine the healing power of the light entering your body and rekindling happiness in you.

For added effect, carve the Sowilo and Ansuz rune on the candle.

Court Case Spells

Court case spells are often used to get a guilty person to walk free. However. To do that you normally need to do black magic and bend the will of the judge. The spells listed here are to help an innocent person so that the judge may see past evil placed on the person, as well as make the person stand in a better light. If you are guilty, these spells may be used to ask for mercy and a lighter sentence.

Simple Tea Light Candle Spell

You can do this spell on the morning of going to court, or start three days before.

Take a white tea light candle and gently remove it from the holder. Anoint it with court case or lavender oil if you cannot get court case oil. Charge the candle by pleading to the judge to be fair and just while also imagining a white light of protection around him/her that the opposition cannot bend the judge's will. Do not try to bend the judge's will by trying to force him/her to rule in your favor, rather treat him/her with the respect they deserve and ask for their assistance if you are truly innocent or their mercy if you are guilty.

You can carve the Tiwaz rune on the candle. Replace the candle to the holder and burn it as you leave to go to court. You can burn one daily for three days before, and then one the day of going to court. For additional effect, you can bathe in court case herbs (or add court case oil to the bathwater) for three days before and the morning of going to court.

Note, tea light candles are used because they naturally are in a protective holder that amplifies the spell as well as protects the spell from interference as well as being cheap and easy to obtain, and easy to hide while being used. You can use normal long white candles if you wish, but they burn longer and cannot be left alone as well as that they are not as protected as tea light candles.

Cotton Ball Spell

If you have no time or place to burn candles, or need added power for your court day, take a cotton ball and gently wet it with court case oil. Place the ball in your bra or pocket during the trial. Furthermore, anoint your pulses (do not use pure essential oil).

Bloodstone Spell

To add power to your other spells, take a bloodstone and anoint it with rosemary water (pour 250 ml of boiling water over a teaspoon of rosemary herbs and let it stand overnight, then strain the water), or use rosemary essential oil. Wrap the stone in a white cloth and tie it closed with a red string or thread while envisioning you winning the case. Carry in your left pocket while at trial.

Use Calendula blossom oil to enhance self-respect and help with a legal victory, as well as slippery elm to protect against false testimony. In addition, place Fiery Wall of Protection oil on your pulses and under the soles of your feet. Add High John the Conqueror herbs or powder to the rosemary water you use to anoint the bloodstone. Or burn High John on charcoal the morning of the trial for added power.

Brown Candle Spell

Take a brown candle and anoint it with court case oil. Carve the Tiwaz rune on the candle. Imagine how you win your court case, then burn the candle. You can do this with the addition of the tea light candles.

Chapter 22: Candle Safety

Candles are open flames, which are alive, destructive, unpredictable, and devious, and must be treated as such. Following are a few safety tips to help you not to burn the house down.

1: Never burn a candle in a non-metal holder not designed for candle burning. Note that many fancy glass candleholders are for display purposes only. Non-metal holders like wood may catch fire, and glass holders may shatter, causing the wick and hot wax to drop through. The wick may continue to burn, and damage the surface below the candle, or cause it to catch fire.
2: Never use a knife or a sharp object to pry out and remove residual wax from a glass holder. Any scratches, even tiny unseen ones, may weaken the glass. Upon your next use, the glass may crack or shatter.
3: Never leave a burning candle alone or go to sleep when one is burning, and make sure the wick ember is no longer glowing when it dies out before leaving it alone.
4: Never trust a thin candle to stand on its own, use a holder.
5: Keep anything that can catch fire at least 1 meter (3 feet) away from the candle. Know that glass candles can explode and normal candles can spit or shoot embers, especially homemade candles.
6: Keep pets and children away from burning candles.
7: Trim the wick down to around ¼ inch before using it.
8: Make sure the candleholder can hold all the wax should the candle melt away instead of burning away.
9: Make sure the surface under the candleholder is heat-resistant, especially on candleholders with flat bottoms. When the candle gets down to the last bit, it can heat the holder up that can cause heat damage to the surface under the holder, even causing glass tables or surfaces to crack.
10: Remove any wick debris from the wax pool under the flame. This can catch fire, causing a second flame that will result in the candle melting down very fast, as well as creating a large and dangerous flame.

11: Do not place candles against each other; leave at least a three-inch gap between candles. Candles placed too close together can create their own draft. This may cause the candles to melt each other. Some spells require candles to be bound together; do expect them to possibly melt away very fast, creating a lot of wax, a large flame, and possibly soot. Plan appropriately.
12: Make sure there is no draft or direct air (ceiling fan or central cooling and heating) blowing near the candle.
13: Do not move a burning candle, and make sure the wax is solid after extinguishing a candle before handling it.
14: Candles use oxygen to burn. Never burn many candles at once in a small room and make sure there is adequate ventilation in the room.
15: Do not use water to extinguish a candle as hot wax can splatter and glass containers can shatter.
16: If a second flame starts on a candle, put it out as the second flame can cause the candle to melt away too fast, catch something on fire, or crack a glass holder. You can use tweezers to remove the second wick.
17: Never put flammable materials (such as wax paper or decorations) around a non-glass container candle. As the flame burns, it will ignite the material, possibly causing a runaway fire that may set other things on fire. At best, your candle will simply melt away very quickly, ruining your spell.
18: If you have to extinguish a candle, use a candlesnuffer. Hot wax may splatter if you blow the flame out, and you may burn your fingers if you pinch the wick.
19: Know that the energy you add to a candle can cause it to burn differently than normal, and differently from other spells that you have done with the same type of candle. Be prepared for all eventualities, a fire can easily start, and destroy your home.

Thank you for taking the time to read ***Candle Magic For Beginners.***

If you enjoyed this book or found it useful, I would be very grateful if you would please post a short review because your support really does make a difference. Alternatively, consider telling your friends about this book because word of mouth is an author's best friend and much appreciated. Thank You.

More Books By Electra

http://valenciacharms.com/books-by-valencia/

Candle Magic For Beginners
Numerology: Discover Why You Are On Earth
Magical Blends
Dragon Book Of Shadows

Made in the USA
Coppell, TX
25 October 2021